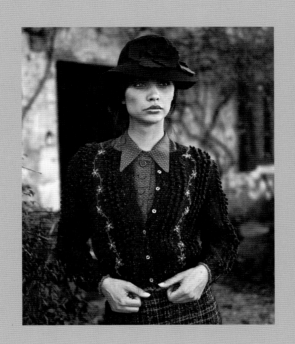

Vintage Knits

30 Knitting Designs from Rowan for Women and Men

Kaffe Fassett · Sarah Dallas · Kim Hargreaves · Martin Storey
Sharon Peake · Louisa Harding · Brandon Mably · Lucinda Guy

TRAFALGAR SQUARE
North Pomfret, Vermont

First published in the United States of America
in 2005 by Trafalgar Square Books
North Pomfret, Vermont 05053
First paperback edition published in 2010

Printed in Singapore

Copyright Rowan Yarns © 2004
First published in Great Britain in 2004 by
Rowan Yarns Ltd, Green Lane Mill, Holmfirth,
West Yorkshire, HD9 2DX

Hand-knit Designers
Kaffe Fassett, Sarah Dallas, Kim Hargreaves,
Martin Storey, Sharon Peake, Louisa Harding,
Brandon Mably, Lucinda Guy

Photographer Joey Toller

Stylist Kim Hargreaves

Hair & Make-up Annabel Hobbs

Models Ivana Filipovic, Nina Hartley
& Charlie Gardner

Designer Simon Wagstaff

Freelance Journalist Alexandra Buxton

Library of Congress Control Number:
2009937557

ISBN: 978-1-57076-458-5

CONTENTS

INTRODUCTION

When we seek comfort and reassurance, we look not
to the future with all its uncertainties but to the past.
Half a century on, the post-war period of the late '40s,
'50s, and '60s seems a golden age when
life was sweetly simple and when time passed with
a less hurried beat.

It's to this era, with its mood of renewal, that we look
for fashion inspiration. After the frugality of the war
years, women rejoiced in wearing swirling skirts, soft
knitwear and exuberant prints. Men, back home once
more and out of their stifling uniforms, relaxed in
turtleneck sweaters and corduroy trousers,
rediscovering the pleasures of color.

To bring this period look alive, this collection draws on
old photographs, films (such as *Chocolat* and *Amélie*),
and archives of knitting patterns. While being true to
the spirit of the age, eight top Bristish hand-knit
designers have updated and adapted classic knits to
make them easy to wear. They have created a look that
exults in happy combinations: old and new, floral and
stripe, texture and sleek.

The collection also encapsulates the feel for quality
materials, for lasting craftsmanship, for classic looks,
and, above all, for a real sense of style. The knitwear
you will find here won't date in the passing of a
season: it will improve with time and become a
treasure in its own right.

Alexandra Buxton

LAURENT
SHARON PEAKE

This little belted jacket, with its small collar, reflects the charm of a quiet French café with its lace curtains and shady interior. The decoration, intarsia flower motifs and embroidery, echoes antique textiles. The jacket works perfectly with a slim-line pleated skirt and delicate blouse. A perky hat completes the look.

LAURENT
SHARON PEAKE

YARN AND SIZES

	XS	S	M	L	XL	
To fit bust	32	34	36	38	40	in
	81	86	91	97	102	cm

Rowan Yorkshire Tweed DK, Yorkshire Tweed 4 ply, and Kid Classic

A = DK—off-white (no. 352) or desired MC

	10	10	11	11	12	x 50g

B = Kid—burgundy (no. 825) or desired 1st CC

	1	1	1	1	1	x 50g

C = DK—scarlet (no. 344) or desired 2nd CC

	1	1	1	1	1	x 50g

D = Kid—terra cotta (no. 827) or desired 3rd CC

	1	1	1	1	1	x 50g

E = 4ply—green (no. 286) or desired 4th CC

	1	1	1	1	1	x 25g

NEEDLES

1 pair size 3 (3¼mm) needles
1 pair size 6 (4mm) needles

EXTRAS—5 buttons (Rowan 00321); and a 1½in/4cm buckle (Rowan 00365)

GAUGE/TENSION

20 sts and 28 rows to 4in/10cm measured over St st using size 6 (4mm) needles.

BACK

Cast on 91 (95: 101: 105: 111) sts using size 3 (3¼mm) needles and yarn A.
Rows 1 and 2: Knit.

Row 3 (RS): K1, *slip 1 st purlwise, K1, rep from * to end.
Row 4: K1, *slip 1 st purlwise with yarn at front (WS) of work, K1, rep from * to end.
Rows 5 and 6: Knit.
Row 7: K2, *slip 1 st purlwise, K1, rep from * to last st, K1.
Row 8: K2, *slip 1 st purlwise with yarn at front (WS) of work, K1, rep from * to last st, K1.
These 8 rows form border patt.
Cont in border patt for 3¼in/8cm, dec 1 st at end of last row and ending with a WS row.
90 (94: 100: 104: 110) sts.
Change to size 6 (4mm) needles.
Beg with a K row, work in St st for 2 rows, ending with a WS row.
Starting and ending rows as indicated and using the **intarsia** technique, cont in patt from chart for back, which is worked entirely in St st beg with a K row, as foll:
Dec 1 st at each end of 5th and foll 6th row.
86 (90: 96: 100: 106) sts.
Work even/straight until chart row 16 has been completed, ending with a WS row.
Break off contrasts and cont in St st using yarn A only.
Dec 1 st at each end of next and foll 6th row.
82 (86: 92: 96: 102) sts.
Work even/straight until back measures 8½ (9: 9: 9½: 9½)in/22 (23: 23: 24: 24)cm, ending with a WS row.

Inc 1 st at each end of next and every foll 10th row until there are 90 (94: 100: 104: 110) sts.
Work 17 rows, ending with a WS row. Back should measure 15¼ (15¾: 15¾: 16¼: 16¼)in/39 (40: 40: 41: 41)cm.

Shape armholes
Bind/cast off 4 (5: 5: 6: 6) sts at beg of next 2 rows. 82 (84: 90: 92: 98) sts.
Dec 1 st at each end of next 5 (5: 7: 7: 9) rows, then on foll 2 alt rows, then on foll 4th row. 66 (68: 70: 72: 74) sts.
Work even/straight until armhole measures 7¾ (7¾: 8¼: 8¼: 8¾)in/20 (20: 21: 21: 22)cm, ending with a WS row.

Shape shoulders and back neck
Bind/cast off 6 (6: 6: 6: 7) sts at beg of next 2 rows. 54 (56: 58: 60: 60) sts.
Next row (RS): Bind/cast off 6 (6: 6: 6: 7) sts, K until there are 10 (10: 11: 11: 10) sts on right needle and turn, leaving rem sts on a holder.
Work each side of neck separately.
Bind/cast off 4 sts at beg of next row.
Bind/cast off rem 6 (6: 7: 7: 6) sts.
With RS facing, rejoin yarn to rem sts,
Bind/cast off center 22 (24: 24: 26: 26) sts, K to end.
Complete to match first side, reversing shapings.

LEFT FRONT

Cast on 51 (53: 57: 59: 61) sts using size 3 (3¼mm) needles and yarn A.

Back chart

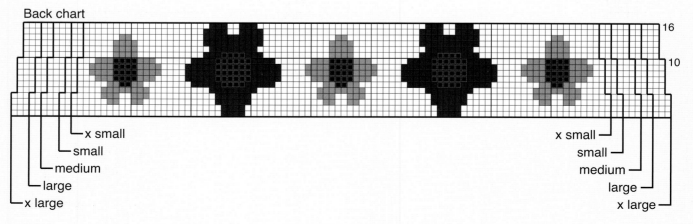

x small
small
medium
large
x large

x small
small
medium
large
x large

Work in border patt as given for back for 3¼in/8cm, ending with a RS row.

Next row (WS): Patt 7 sts and slip these sts onto a holder, M1, patt to last 0 (0: 2: 2: 0) sts, (K2tog) 0 (0: 1: 1: 0) times.

45 (47: 50: 52: 55) sts.

Change to size 6 (4mm) needles.

Beg with a K row, work in St st for 4 rows, ending with a WS row.

Starting and ending rows as indicated, cont in patt from chart for lower left front as foll:

Dec 1 st at beg of 3rd and every foll 6th row until 42 (44: 47: 49: 52) sts rem.

Work even/straight until chart row 18 has been completed, ending with a WS row.

Break off contrasting yarns and cont in St st using yarn A only.

Dec 1 st at beg of 3rd row. 41 (43: 46: 48: 51) sts.

Work even/straight until left front measures 8½ (9: 9: 9½: 9½)in/22 (23: 23: 24: 24)cm, ending with a WS row.

Inc 1 st at beg of next and foll 10th row.

43 (45: 48: 50: 53) sts.

Work 7 rows, ending with a WS row.

Place Chart

Next row (RS): Using yarn A, K17 (19: 22: 24: 27); work last 26 sts as row 1 of chart for upper left front.

Next row: Work first 26 sts as row 2 of chart for upper left front; using yarn A, P to end.

These 2 rows set position of chart with side edge sts in St st using yarn A.

Working rem 58 rows of chart, then completing

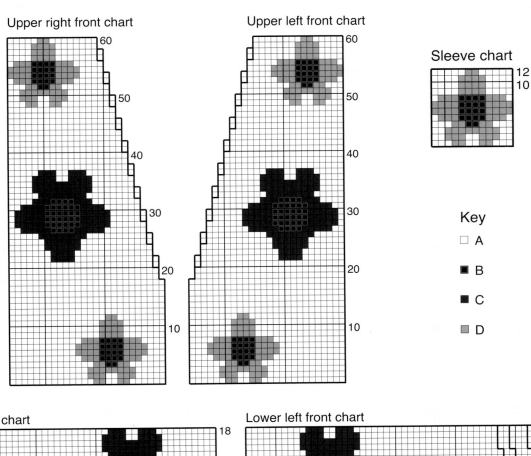

Upper right front chart

Upper left front chart

Sleeve chart

Key

□ A

■ B

■ C

■ D

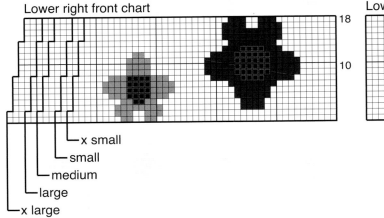

Lower right front chart

x small
small
medium
large
x large

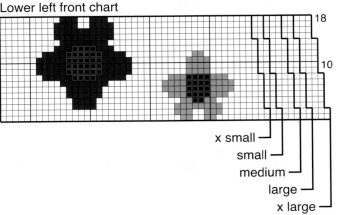

Lower left front chart

x small
small
medium
large
x large

11

work in St st using yarn A only, cont as foll:

Inc 1 st at beg of next and foll 10th row.

45 (47: 50: 52: 55) sts.

Work 5 rows, ending with a WS row.

Shape front slope

Keeping patt correct, dec 1 st at end of next and foll 0 (0: 0: 1: 0) alt rows, then on every foll 4th row until 42 (44: 47: 48: 52) sts rem.

Work 3 (3: 3: 1: 3) rows, ending with a WS row. (Left front now matches back to beg of armhole shaping.)

Shape armhole

Keeping patt correct, bind/cast off 4 (5: 5: 6: 6) sts at beg and dec 1 (1: 1: 0: 1) st at end of next row. 37 (38: 41: 42: 45) sts.

Work 1 row.

Dec 1 st at armhole edge of next 5 (5: 7: 7: 9) rows, then on foll 2 alt rows, then on foll 4th row **and at same time** dec 1 st at front slope edge on 3rd (3rd: 3rd: next: 3rd) and every foll 4th row. 26 (27: 27: 28: 29) sts.

Dec 1 st at front slope edge only on 2nd (2nd: 4th: 2nd: 2nd) and every foll 4th row to 20 (18: 20: 19: 21) sts, then on every foll 6th (-: 6th: -: 6th) row until 18 (-: 19: -: 20) sts rem.

Work even/straight until left front matches back to start of shoulder shaping, ending with WS row.

Shape shoulder

Bind/cast off 6 (6: 6: 6: 7) sts at beg of next and foll alt row. Work 1 row.

Bind/cast off rem 6 (6: 7: 7: 6) sts.

RIGHT FRONT

Cast on 51 (53: 57: 59: 61) sts using size 3 (3¹/₄mm) needles and yarn A.

Work in border patt as given for back for 3¹/₄in/8cm, ending with a RS row.

Next row (WS): (K2tog) 0 (0: 1: 1: 0) times, patt to last 7 sts, M1 and turn, leaving rem 7 sts on a holder. 45 (47: 50: 52: 55) sts.

Change to size 6 (4mm) needles.

Beg with a K row, work in St st for 4 rows, ending with a WS row.

Starting and ending rows as indicated, cont in patt from chart for lower right front as foll:

Dec 1 st at end of 3rd and every foll 6th row until 42 (44: 47: 49: 52) sts rem.

Work even/straight until chart row 18 has been completed, ending with a WS row.

Break off contrasting yarns and cont in St st using yarn A only.

Dec 1 st at end of 3rd row. 41 (43: 46: 48: 51) sts.

Work even/straight until right front measures 8¹/₂ (9: 9: 9¹/₂: 9¹/₂)in/22 (23: 23: 24: 24)cm, ending with a WS row.

Inc 1 st at end of next and foll 10th row. 43 (45: 48: 50: 53) sts.

Place Chart

Work 7 rows, ending with a WS row.

Next row (RS): Work first 26 sts as row 1 of chart for upper right front; using yarn A, K to end.

Next row: Using yarn A, P17 (19: 22: 24: 27); work last 26 sts as row 2 of chart for upper right front.

These 2 rows set position of chart with side edge sts in St st using yarn A.

Working rem 58 rows of chart, then completing work in St st using yarn A only, complete to match left front, reversing shapings.

SLEEVES (both alike)

Cast on 53 (53: 55: 57: 57) sts using size 3 (3¹/₄mm) needles and yarn A.

Work in border patt as given for back, dec 1 st at each end of 9th and every foll 6th row until 47 (47: 49: 51: 51) sts rem.

Work 4 rows more, dec 1 st at end of last row and ending with a RS row.

46 (46: 48: 50: 50) sts.

Place markers at both ends of last row.

Change to size 6 (4mm) needles.

Beg with a K row (to reverse RS of work), cont in St st, shaping sides by inc 1 st at each end of 9th (7th: 7th: 7th: 7th) and foll 10th (8th: 8th: 8th: 8th) row. 50 (50: 52: 54: 54) sts.

Place Chart

Work 3 (7: 7: 7: 7) rows, ending with a WS row.

Next row (RS): Using yarn A, (inc in first st) 0 (1: 0: 0: 1) times, K19 (18: 20: 21: 20); work next 12 sts as row 1 of chart for sleeve; using yarn A, K to last 0 (1: 0: 0: 1) st, (inc in last st) 0 (1: 0: 0: 1) times. 50 (52: 52: 54: 56) sts.

Next row: Using yarn A, 19 (20: 20: 21: 22); work next 12 sts as row 2 of chart for sleeve; using yarn A, P to end.

These 2 rows set position of chart with sts on each side in St st using yarn A.

Cont as set, inc 1 st at each end of 5th (9th: next: next: 7th) row. 52 (54: 54: 56: 58) sts.

Work 5 (1: 9: 9: 3) rows more, completing chart row 12 and ending with a WS row.

Break off contrasting yarns and cont using yarn A only.

Inc 1 st at each end of 5th (9th: next: next: 5th) and every foll 10th (10th: 10th: 10th: 8th) row to 62 (68: 70: 72: 64) sts, then on every foll 12th (-: -: -: 10th) row until there are 66 (-: -: -: 74) sts.

Work even/straight until sleeve measures 16¹/₂ (16¹/₂: 17: 17: 17)in/42 (42: 43: 43: 43)cm from markers, ending with a WS row.

Shape sleeve cap

Bind/cast off 4 (5: 5: 6: 6) sts at beg of next 2 rows. 58 (58: 60: 60: 62) sts.

Dec 1 st at each end of next 5 rows, then on foll 2 alt rows, then on every foll 4th row until 36 (36: 38: 38: 40) sts rem.

Work 1 row, ending with a WS row.

Dec 1 st at each end of next and every foll alt row to 28 sts, then on foll 3 rows, ending with a WS row. Bind/cast off rem 22 sts.

FINISHING

PRESS as described on page 136.

Join both shoulder seams using backstitch.

Button band and left collar

Slip 7 sts from left front holder onto size 3 (3¹/₄mm) needles and rejoin yarn A with RS facing.

Cont in border patt until band, when slightly stretched, fits up left front opening edge to start of front slope shaping, ending with a WS row.

Inc 1 st at beg of next and every foll 4th row until there are 28 sts, taking inc sts into patt.

Work even/straight until this collar section, unstretched, fits up left front slope and across to center back neck. Bind/cast off.

Mark positions for 5 buttons on this band—first to come just above border patt, last to come just below start of front slope shaping, and rem 3 buttons evenly spaced between.

Buttonhole band and right collar

Slip 7 sts from right front holder onto size 3 (3^1/4mm) needles and rejoin yarn A with WS facing. Work 1 row.

Next row (buttonhole row) (RS): Patt 2 sts, work 2 tog, yo, patt to end.

Working 4 buttonholes more to correspond with positions marked on left front for buttons, complete to match button band and left collar, reversing shapings. Join center back seam of collar sections, then slip stitch bands and collar in place.

Embroidery

Using yarn E and diagrams as a guide, embroider chain stitch lines onto all pieces.

See page 136 for finishing instructions, setting in sleeves using the set-in method and reversing sleeve seam below markers for turn-back.

Belt

Cast on 9 sts using size 3 (3^1/4mm) needles and yarn A.

Work in border patt as given for back for 27^1/2 (29^1/2: 31^1/2: 33^1/2: 35^1/2)in/70 (75: 80: 85: 90)cm. Bind/cast off.

Attach buckle to one end of belt.

Chain Stitch

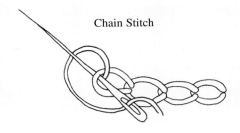

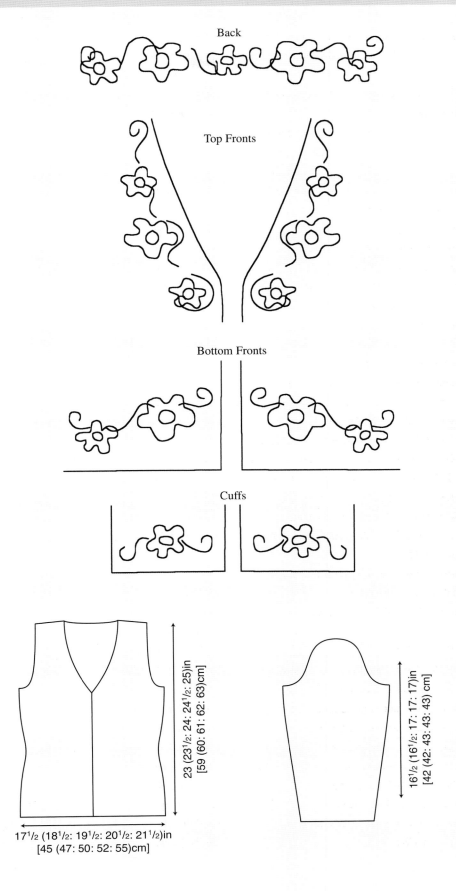

Back

Top Fronts

Bottom Fronts

Cuffs

23 (23^1/2: 24: 24^1/2: 25)in [59 (60: 61: 62: 63)cm]

17^1/2 (18^1/2: 19^1/2: 20^1/2: 21^1/2)in [45 (47: 50: 52: 55)cm]

16^1/2 (16^1/2: 17: 17: 17)in [42 (42: 43: 43: 43) cm]

CHINESE BASKET
KAFFE FASSETT

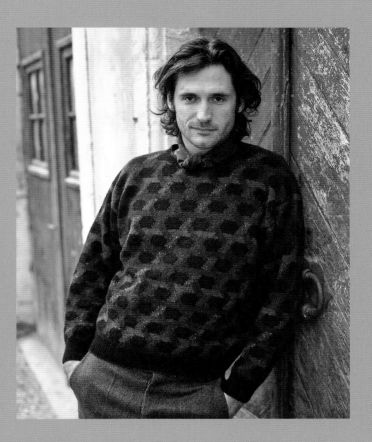

The crisscrossing of rich dark colors create a
masculine look in this geometric sweater and pullover.
Ruggedly handsome, these knits take their color and
design inspiration from nature: woods and farms,
ploughed fields and log piles, stacked up in preparation
for winter months ahead.

CHINESE BASKET
KAFFE FASSETT

YARN AND SIZES

	S	M	L	XL	XXL	
To fit chest	38	40	42	44	46	in
	97	102	107	112	117	cm

Rowan Yorkshire Tweed 4 ply

SWEATER

A = black (no. 283) or desired MC

	9	9	9	10	10	x 25g

B = dark green (no. 282) or desired 1st CC

	3	3	3	3	3	x 25g

C = charcoal (no. 277) or desired 2nd CC

	3	3	3	3	3	x 25g

D = dark red (no. 279) or desired 3rd CC

	5	5	6	6	6	x 25g

E = dark blue (no. 281) or desired 4th CC

	3	3	3	3	4	x 25g

F = medium purple (no. 276) or desired 5th CC

	3	3	3	3	3	x 25g

G = dark rust (no. 278) or desired 6th CC

	2	2	2	3	3	x 25g

PULLOVER

A = black (no. 283) or desired MC

	4	4	5	5	5	x 25g

B = dark green (no. 282) or desired 1st CC

	2	2	2	2	2	x 25g

C = charcoal (no. 277) or desired 2nd CC

	2	2	2	2	2	x 25g

D = dark red (no. 279) or desired 3rd CC

	2	2	2	2	2	x 25g

E = dark blue (no. 281) or desired 4th CC

	2	2	2	2	2	x 25g

F = medium purple (no. 276) or desired 5th CC

	2	2	2	2	2	x 25g

G = dark rust (no. 278) or desired 6th CC

	2	2	2	2	2	x 25g

NEEDLES

1 pair size 1 (2^1/4mm) needles
1 pair size 2 (3mm) needles

GAUGE/TENSION

28 sts and 40 rows to 4in/10cm measured over patterned St st using size 2 (3mm) needles.

SPECIAL CHART/KEY NOTE

The colors on the chart correspond to the yarns as foll:

A = black squares (background)
B = turquoise squares (diagonal stripes)
C = white squares (diagonal stripes)
D = grape squares (diagonal stripes)
E = blue squares (horizontal stripes)
F = lilac squares (horizontal stripes)
G = rust squares (horizontal stripes)

SWEATER

BACK

Cast on 157 (163: 171: 177: 185) sts using size 1 (2^1/4mm) needles and yarn E.
Break off yarn E and join in yarn A.
Row 1 (RS): K1, *P1, K1, rep from * to end.
Row 2: P1, *K1, P1, rep from * to end.
These 2 rows form rib.
Cont in rib for 2^1/2in/6cm, inc 1 st at end of last row and ending with a WS row.
158 (164: 172: 178: 186) sts.
Change to size 2 (3mm) needles.
Starting and ending rows as indicated, using the **intarsia** technique and repeating the 108 row patt repeat throughout, cont in patt from chart, which is worked entirely in St st beg with a K row, as foll:
Work even/straight until back measures 13^3/4 (13^3/4: 14^1/4: 14^1/4: 14^3/4)in/35 (35: 36: 36: 37)cm, ending with a WS row.
Shape armholes
Keeping patt correct, bind/cast off 7 sts at beg of next 2 rows. 144 (150: 158: 164: 172) sts.
Dec 1 st at each end of next 5 rows.
134 (140: 148: 154: 162) sts.
Work even/straight until armhole measures 9^3/4 (10^1/4: 10^1/4: 10^1/2: 10^1/2)in/25 (26: 26: 27: 27)cm, ending with a WS row.
Shape shoulders and back neck
Bind/cast off 13 (14: 15: 16: 17) sts at beg of next 2 rows. 108 (112: 118: 122: 128) sts.

Next row (RS): Bind/cast off 13 (14: 15: 16: 17) sts, patt until there are 18 (18: 20: 20: 21) sts on right needle and turn, leaving rem sts on a holder.
Work each side of neck separately.
Bind/cast off 4 sts at beg of next row.
Bind/cast off rem 14 (14: 16: 16: 17) sts.
With RS facing, rejoin yarns to rem sts, bind/cast off center 46 (48: 48: 50: 52) sts, patt to end.
Complete to match first side, reversing shapings.

FRONT

Work as given for back until 24 (24: 26: 26: 26) rows less have been worked than on back to start of shoulder shaping, end with a WS row.
Shape neck
Next row (RS): Patt 57 (59: 64: 66: 69) sts and turn, leaving rem sts on a holder.
Work each side of neck separately.
Bind/cast off 4 sts at beg of next and foll alt row. 49 (51: 56: 58: 61) sts.
Dec 1 st at neck edge of next 5 rows, then on foll 2 (2: 3: 3: 3) alt rows, then on every foll 4th row until 40 (42: 46: 48: 51) sts rem.
Work 3 rows, ending with a WS row.
Shape shoulder
Bind/cast off 13 (14: 15: 16: 17) sts at beg of next and foll alt row.
Work 1 row. Bind/cast off rem 14 (14: 16: 16: 17) sts.
With RS facing, rejoin yarns to rem sts, bind/cast off center 20 (22: 20: 22: 24) sts, patt to end.
Complete to match first side, reversing shapings.

SLEEVES (both alike)

Cast on 79 (79: 81: 83: 83) sts using size 1 (2^1/4mm) needles and yarn E.
Break off yarn E and join in yarn A.
Work in rib as given for back for 2^1/2in/6cm, inc 1 st at end of last row and ending with a WS row. 80 (80: 82: 84: 84) sts.

Change to size 2 (3mm) needles.

Starting and ending rows as indicated, cont in patt from chart, shaping sides by inc 1 st at each end of 5th and every foll 6th row to 104 (96: 102: 100: 100) sts, then on every foll 4th row until there are 140 (146: 146: 152: 152) sts, taking inc sts into patt.

Work even/straight until sleeve measures 19 (19^1/$_4$: 19^1/$_4$: 19^1/$_2$: 19^1/$_2$)in/48 (49: 49: 50: 50)cm, ending with a WS row.

Shape top of sleeve

Keeping patt correct, bind/cast off 7 sts at beg of next 2 rows. 126 (132: 132: 138: 138) sts.

Dec 1 st at each end of next and foll 6 alt rows.

Work 1 row, ending with a WS row.

Bind/cast off rem 112 (118: 118: 124: 124) sts.

FINISHING

PRESS as described on page 136.

Join right shoulder seam using backstitch.

Neckband

With RS facing, using size 1 (2^1/$_4$mm) needles and yarn A, pick up and knit 30 (30: 32: 32: 32) sts down left side of neck, 19 (21: 19: 21: 23) sts from front, 30 (30: 32: 32: 32) sts up right side of neck, then 54 (56: 56: 58: 60) sts from back. 133 (137: 139: 143: 147) sts.

Work in rib as given for back for 9 rows.

Break off yarn A and join in yarn E.

Work 1 row. Bind/cast off in rib (on WS).

See page 136 for finishing instructions, setting in sleeves using the shallow set-in method.

PULLOVER

BACK

Cast on 145 (151: 159: 165: 173) sts using size 1 (2^1/$_4$mm) needles and yarn E.

Break off yarn E and join in yarn A.

Row 1 (RS): K1, *P1, K1, rep from * to end.

Row 2: P1, *K1, P1, rep from * to end.

These 2 rows form rib.

Cont in rib for 2^1/$_2$in/6cm, inc 1 st at end of last

row and ending with a WS row. 146 (152: 160: 166: 174) sts.

Change to size 2 (3mm) needles.

Starting and ending rows as indicated, using the **intarsia** technique and repeating the 108 row patt repeat throughout, cont in patt from chart, which is worked entirely in St st beg with a K row, as foll:

Work even/straight until back measures 13^3/$_4$ (13^3/$_4$: 14^1/$_4$: 14^1/$_4$: 14^3/$_4$)in/35 (35: 36: 36: 37)cm, ending with a WS row.

Shape armholes

Keeping patt correct, bind/cast off 6 (7: 7: 8: 8) sts at beg of next 2 rows.

134 (138: 146: 150: 158) sts.**

Dec 1 st at each end of next 7 (7: 9: 9: 11) rows, then on foll 4 (5: 5: 6: 6) alt rows, then on every foll 4th row until 108 (110: 114: 116: 120) sts rem.

Work even/straight until armhole measures 9^3/$_4$ (10^1/$_4$: 10^1/$_4$: 10^1/$_2$: 10^1/$_2$)in/25 (26: 26: 27: 27)cm, ending with a WS row.

Shape shoulders and back neck

Bind/cast off 10 (10: 11: 11: 11) sts at beg of next 2 rows. 88 (90: 92: 94: 98) sts.

Next row (RS): Bind/cast off 10 (10: 11: 11: 11) sts, patt until there are 14 (14: 14: 14: 15) sts on right needle and turn, leaving rem sts on a holder.

Work each side of neck separately.

Bind/cast off 4 sts at beg of next row.

Bind/cast off rem 10 (10: 10: 10: 11) sts.

With RS facing, rejoin yarns to rem sts, bind/cast off center 40 (42: 42: 44: 46) sts, patt to end.

Complete to match first side, reversing shapings.

FRONT

Work as given for back to **.

Dec 1 st at each end of next 6 rows, ending with a WS row. 122 (126: 134: 138: 146) sts.

Divide for neck

Next row (RS): K2tog, patt 57 (59: 63:

65: 69) sts, K2tog and turn, leaving rem sts on a holder.

Work each side of neck separately.

Dec 0 (0: 1: 1: 1) st at armhole edge of next row. 59 (61: 64: 66: 70) sts.

Dec 1 st at armhole edge of next 1 (1: 1: 1: 3) rows, then on foll 3 (4: 5: 6: 6) alt rows, then on 2 foll 4th rows **and at same time** dec 1 st at neck edge on next and every foll alt row. 45 (45: 46: 46: 47) sts.

Dec 1 st at neck edge only on 2nd (2nd: 2nd: 4th: 2nd) and foll 2 (1: 0: 0: 0) alt rows, then on every foll 4th row to 35 (35: 37: 37: 38) sts, then on every foll 6th row until 30 (30: 32: 32: 33) sts rem.

Work even/straight until front matches back to start of shoulder shaping, ending with WS row.

Shape shoulder

Bind/cast off 10 (10: 11: 11: 11) sts at beg of next and foll alt row.

Work 1 row. Bind/cast off rem 10 (10: 10: 10: 11) sts.

With RS facing, rejoin yarns to rem sts, K2tog, patt to last 2 sts, K2tog.

Complete to match first side, reversing shapings.

FINISHING

PRESS as described on page 136.

Join right shoulder seam using backstitch.

Neckband

With RS facing, using size 1 (2^1/$_4$mm) needles and yarn A, pick up and knit 78 (80: 80: 84: 84) sts down left side of neck, one st from base of V (mark this st with a colored thread), 78 (80: 80: 84: 84) sts up right side of neck, then 48 (50: 50: 52: 54) sts from back. 205 (211: 211: 221: 223) sts.

Row 1 (WS): P1, *K1, P1, rep from * to end.

This row sets position of rib.

Keeping rib correct, cont as foll:

Row 2: Rib to within 2 sts of marked st, K2tog tbl, K marked st, K2tog, rib to end.

CHINESE BASKET
KAFFE FASSETT

108 row patt repeat

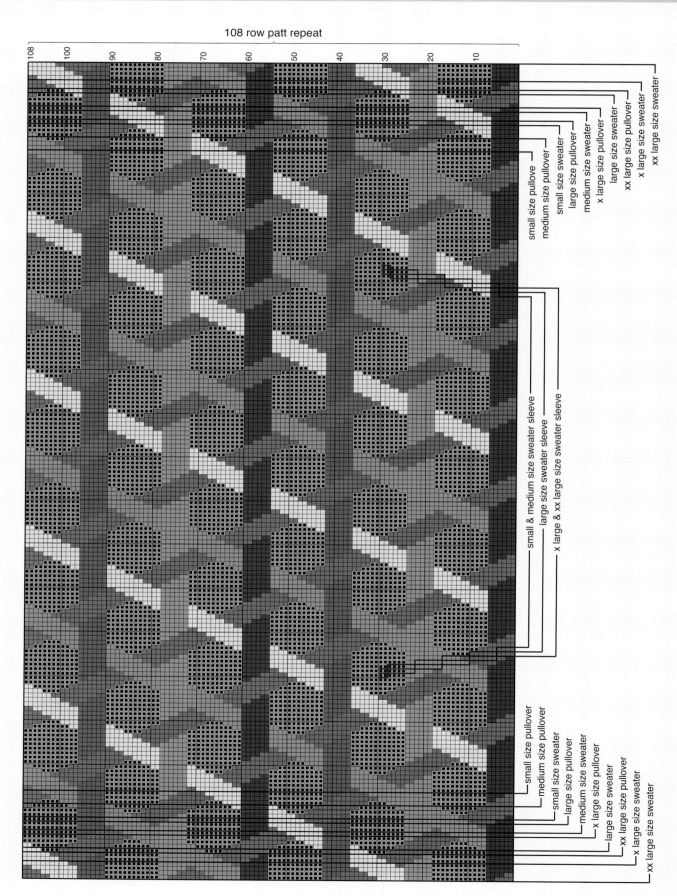

small size pullove
medium size pullover
small size sweater
large size pullover
medium size sweater
x large size pullover
large size sweater
xx large size pullover
x large size sweater
xx large size sweater

small & medium size sweater sleeve
large size sweater sleeve
x large & xx large size sweater sleeve

small size pullover
medium size pullover
small size sweater
large size pullover
medium size sweater
x large size pullover
large size sweater
xx large size pullover
x large size sweater
xx large size sweater

Row 3: Rib to marked st, P marked st, rib to end.

Rep last 2 rows 3 times more.

197 (203: 203: 213: 215) sts.

Break off yarn A and join in yarn E.

Row 10: As row 2.

Bind/cast off in rib (on WS).

Join left shoulder and neckband seam.

Armhole borders (both alike)

With RS facing, using size 1 (2¼mm) needles and yarn A, pick up and knit 159 (167: 167: 175: 175) sts around armhole edge.

Work in rib as given for back for 7 rows.

Break off yarn A and join in yarn E.

Work 1 row. Bind/cast off in rib (on WS).

See page 136 for finishing instructions.

SWEATER

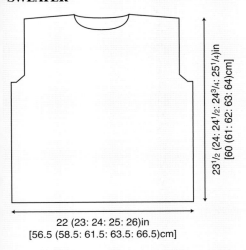

23½ (24: 24½: 24¾: 25¼)in
[60 (61: 62: 63: 64)cm]

22 (23: 24: 25: 26)in
[56.5 (58.5: 61.5: 63.5: 66.5)cm]

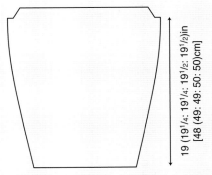

19 (19¼: 19¼: 19½: 19½)in
[48 (49: 49: 50: 50)cm]

PULLOVER

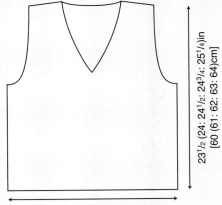

23½ (24: 24½: 24¾: 25¼)in
[60 (61: 62: 63: 64)cm]

20½ (21½: 22½: 23½: 24½)in
[52 (54.5: 57: 59.5: 62)cm]

Suzette

KIM HARGREAVES

This striped cardigan has a disarming innocence, knitted up in blues, browns, and naturals, and worn here with an open-necked blouse. The stripes are interspersed with rows of folkloric motifs, inspired by craft knitwear. It's a gentle look redolent of weekends in the country, precious time away from the hustle-bustle of the city.

YARN AND SIZES

	XS	S	M	L	XL	
To fit bust	32	34	36	38	40	in
	81	86	91	97	102	cm

Rowan Yorkshire Tweed 4 ply

A = light gray (no. 270) or desired 1st CC

	4	4	5	5	5	x 25g

B = medium purple (no. 276) or desired 2nd CC

	2	2	2	2	2	x 25g

C = red (no. 275) or desired 3rd CC

	1	1	1	1	1	x 25g

D = light green (no. 272) or desired 4th CC

	1	1	1	1	2	x 25g

E = charcoal (no. 277) or desired 5th CC

	2	2	2	2	2	x 25g

F = rose (no. 269) or desired 6th CC

	2	2	2	2	2	x 25g

G = medium gray (no. 266) or desired 7th CC

	2	2	2	2	2	x 25g

H = gray-blue (no. 267) or desired 8th CC

	2	2	2	2	2	x 25g

J = gray-lilac (no. 268) or desired 9th CC

	2	2	2	2	2	x 25g

NEEDLES AND CROCHET HOOK

1 pair size 3 (3 1/4 mm) needles

Size D-3 (3.25mm) crochet hook

BUTTONS—9 buttons (Rowan 00315)

GAUGE/TENSION

30 sts and 37 rows to 4in/10cm measured over patterned St st using size 3 (3 1/4 mm) needles.

CROCHET ABBREVIATIONS

sc = single crochet (double crochet UK)

ch = chain.

BACK

Cast on 119 (127: 135: 143: 151) sts using size 3 (3 1/4 mm) needles and yarn A.

Starting and ending rows as indicated and using the **Fair Isle** technique, cont in patt from chart for body, which is worked entirely in St st beg with a K row, as foll:

Dec 1 st at each end of 23rd (25th: 25th: 27th: 27th) and every foll 6th row until 107 (115: 123: 131: 139) sts rem.

Work 15 (17: 17: 19: 19) rows, ending with a WS row.

Inc 1 st at each end of next and every foll 8th row to 119 (127: 135: 143: 151) sts, then on every foll 6th row until there are 125 (133: 141: 149: 157) sts, taking inc sts into patt.

Work even/straight until chart row 136 (140: 140: 144: 144) has been completed, ending with a WS row. Back should measure 14 3/4 (15: 15: 15 1/2: 15 1/2)in/37 (38: 38: 39: 39)cm.

Shape armholes

Keeping patt correct, bind/cast off 4 (5: 5: 6: 6) sts at beg of next 2 rows. 117 (123: 131: 137: 145) sts.

Dec 1 st at each end of next 7 (7: 9: 9: 11) rows, then on foll 4 (5: 5: 6: 6) alt rows. 95 (99: 103: 107: 111) sts.

Work even/straight until chart row 214 (218: 222: 226: 230) has been completed, ending with a WS row. Armhole should measure 8 1/4 (8 1/4: 8 1/2: 8 1/2: 9)in/21 (21: 22: 22: 23)cm.

Shape shoulders and back neck

Bind/cast off 8 (9: 9: 10: 10) sts at beg of next 2 rows. 79 (81: 85: 87: 91) sts.

Next row (RS): Bind/cast off 8 (9: 9: 10: 10) sts, patt until there are 13 (12: 14: 13: 15) sts on right needle and turn, leaving rem sts on a holder.

Work each side of neck separately.

Bind/cast off 4 sts at beg of next row.

Bind/cast off rem 9 (8: 10: 9: 11) sts.

With RS facing, rejoin yarns to rem sts, bind/cast off center 37 (39: 39: 41: 41) sts, patt to end.

Complete to match first side, reversing shapings.

LEFT FRONT

Cast on 60 (64: 68: 72: 76) sts using size 3 (3 1/4 mm) needles and yarn A.

Starting and ending rows as indicated, cont in patt from chart for body as foll:

Dec 1 st at beg of 23rd (25th: 25th: 27th: 27th) and every foll 6th row until 54 (58: 62: 66: 70) sts rem.

Work 15 (17: 17: 19: 19) rows, ending with a WS row.

Inc 1 st at beg of next and every foll 8th row to 60 (64: 68: 72: 76) sts, then on every foll 6th row until there are 63 (67: 71: 75: 79) sts, taking inc sts into patt.

Work even/straight until left front matches back to beg of armhole shaping, ending with a WS row.

Shape armhole

Keeping patt correct, bind/cast off 4 (5: 5: 6: 6) sts at beg of next row. 59 (62: 66: 69: 73) sts.

Work 1 row.

Dec 1 st at each end of next 7 (7: 9: 9: 11) rows, then on foll 3 (3: 2: 2: 1) alt rows.

49 (52: 55: 58: 61) sts.

Work 1 row, ending with a WS row.

Shape front slope

Keeping patt correct, dec 1 st at each end of next and foll 0 (1: 2: 3: 4) alt rows.

47 (48: 49: 50: 51) sts.

Dec 1 st at front slope edge only on 2nd and foll 17 (18: 15: 16: 13) alt rows, then on every foll 4th row until 25 (26: 28: 29: 31) sts rem.

Work even/straight until left front matches back to start of shoulder shaping, ending with a WS row.

Shape shoulder

Bind/cast off 8 (9: 9: 10: 10) sts at beg of next and foll alt row.

Work 1 row.

Bind/cast off rem 9 (8: 10: 9: 11) sts.

RIGHT FRONT

Work to match left front, reversing shapings.

SLEEVES (both alike)

Cast on 77 (77: 79: 81: 81) sts using size 3

(3¹/4mm) needles and yarn A.

Starting and ending rows as indicated and beg with chart row 1 (5: 1: 5: 5), cont in patt from chart for sleeve as foll:

Inc 1 st at each end of 15th row, taking inc sts into patt. 79 (79: 81: 83: 83) sts.

Work 11 (7: 11: 7: 7) rows more, ending with chart row 26 and a WS row.

Starting and ending rows as indicated, cont in patt from chart for body as foll:

Inc 1 st at each end of 5th (7th: 3rd: 7th: 5th) and every foll 16th (14th: 12th: 12th: 12th) row to 83 (89: 103: 105: 87) sts, then on every foll 14th (12th: -: -: 10th) row until there are 97 (99: -: -: 109) sts, taking inc sts into patt.

Work even/straight until chart row 136 (140: 140: 144: 144) has been completed, ending with a WS row. Sleeve to measure 17¹/4 (17¹/4: 17¹/2: 17¹/2: 17¹/2)in/45 (45: 46: 46: 46)cm.

Shape sleeve cap

Keeping patt correct, bind/cast off 4 (5: 5: 6: 6) sts at beg of next 2 rows. 89 (89: 93: 93: 97)sts.

Dec 1 st at each end of next 3 rows, then on foll 2 alt rows, then on every foll 4th row until 59 (59: 63: 63: 67) sts rem.

Work 1 row, ending with a WS row.

Dec 1 st at each end of next and every foll alt row to 55 sts, then on foll 7 rows, ending with a WS row. Bind/cast off rem 41 sts.

FINISHING

PRESS as described on page 136.

Join both shoulder seams using backstitch, or mattress stitch. See page 136 for finishing instructions, setting in sleeves using the set-in method.

Mark positions for 9 buttonholes along right front opening edge—first buttonhole ¹/2in/1cm up from cast-on edge, last buttonhole just below start of front slope shaping, and rem 7 buttonholes evenly spaced between.

Edging

Using size D-3 (3.25mm) crochet hook and yarn A, attach yarn to base of right side seam and work 1 round of sc evenly around entire hem, front opening and neck edges, working 2sc in corners, ensuring edging lays flat and ending with a slip st in first sc.

Break off yarn A and join in yarn C.

Next round: Ch1 (does NOT count as st), 1sc in each sc to end, working extra sc at corners and skipping sc as required along slopes to ensure edging lays flat, join with a slip st in first sc.

Break off yarn C and join in yarn E.

Rep last round once more, making buttonholes at positions marked by replacing (1sc in each of next 2sc) with (ch2, skip 2sc). Fasten off.

In same way, work edging around cast-on edge of sleeves.

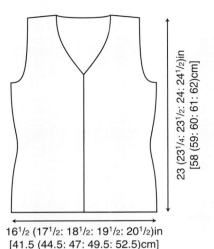

23 (23¹/4: 23¹/2: 24: 24¹/2)in [58 (59: 60: 61: 62)cm]

16¹/2 (17¹/2: 18¹/2: 19¹/2: 20¹/2)in [41.5 (44.5: 47: 49.5: 52.5)cm]

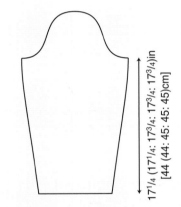

17¹/4 (17¹/4: 17¹/2: 17³/4: 17³/4)in [44 (44: 45: 45: 45)cm]

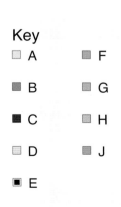

Key

☐	A	▨	F
▨	B	☐	G
■	C	☐	H
☐	D	▨	J
▨	E		

Sleeve chart

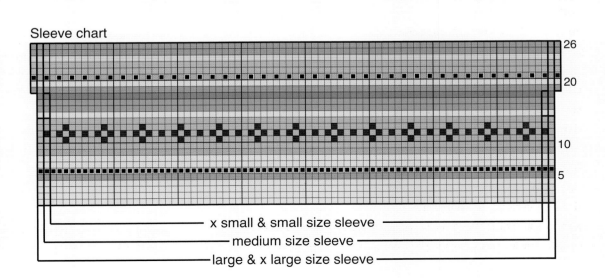

26
20
10
5

x small & small size sleeve
medium size sleeve
large & x large size sleeve

Suzette

KIM HARGREAVES

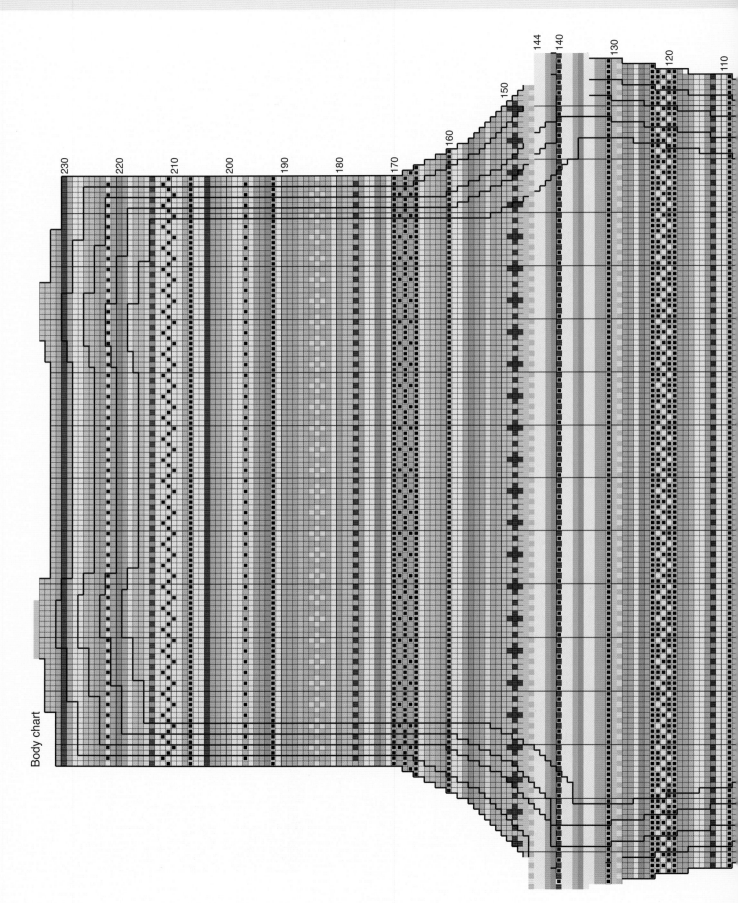

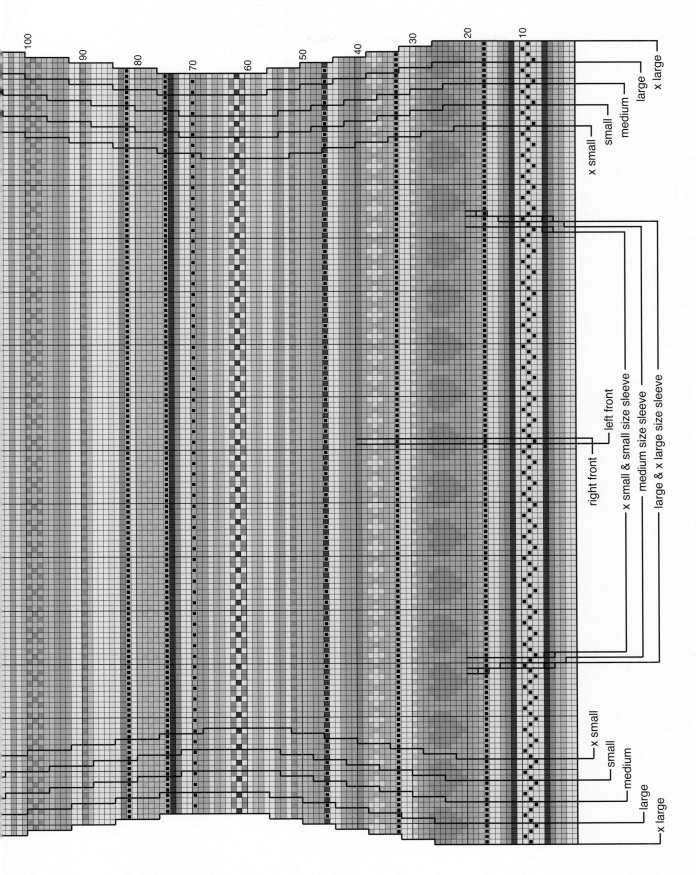

100

90

80

70

60

50

40

30

20

10

x small
small
medium
large
x large

right front
left front
x small & small size sleeve
medium size sleeve
large & x large size sleeve

x small
small
medium
large
x large

FLEUR
KIM HARGREAVES

Elegant and feminine, this cardigan is a real gem. The beautiful beaded detail around
the edging and cuffs emphasizes the simple, curving shape. The attention to detail takes
us back to an artisan era, before the advent of mass production, when garments were
chosen with the greatest care and stored in tissue paper.

FLEUR
KIM HARGREAVES

YARN AND SIZES

	XS	S	M	L	XL	
To fit bust	32	34	36	38	40	in
	81	86	91	97	102	cm

Rowan 4 ply Soft

	6	7	7	8	8	x 50g

Use gray-green (no. 367) or desired color

NEEDLES

1 pair size 2 (2³/₄mm) needles
1 pair size 3 (3¹/₄mm) needles

EXTRAS—1 hook and eye; and approx 800 beads (Rowan 01020)

GAUGE/TENSION

28 sts and 36 rows to 4in/10cm measured over St st using size 3 (3¹/₄mm) needles.

SPECIAL ABBREVIATIONS

Bead 1 = place a bead by bringing yarn to front (RS) of work and slipping bead up next to st just worked, slip next st purlwise from left needle to right needle and take yarn back to back (WS) of work, leaving bead sitting in front of slipped st on RS.

Beading note: Before starting to knit, thread beads onto yarn. To do this, thread a fine sewing needle (one that will easily pass through the beads) with sewing thread. Knot ends of thread and then pass end of yarn through this loop. Thread a bead onto sewing thread and then gently slide it along and onto knitting yarn. Continue in this way until required number of beads are on yarn.

BACK

Cast on 102 (108: 116: 122: 130) sts using size 3 (3¹/₄mm) needles.
Beg with a K row, work in St st for 10 rows, ending with a WS row.
Inc 1 st at each end of next and foll 10th row, then on foll 8th row, then on foll 6th row, then on every foll 4th row until there are 116 (122: 130: 136: 144) sts.
Work 1 row, ending with a WS row.
Inc 1 st at each end of next and foll 5 alt rows, then on foll 5 rows, ending with a WS row.
138 (144: 152: 158: 166) sts.
Cast on 3 sts at beg of next 6 rows, 4 sts at beg of foll 12 rows, 6 sts at beg of next 2 rows, 8 sts at beg of foll 4 rows, 10 sts at beg of next 2 rows, 18 sts at beg of foll 2 rows, and then 18 (18: 21: 21: 21) sts at beg of next 2 rows.
340 (346: 360: 366: 374) sts.
Work even/straight until back measures 4³/₄ (4³/₄: 5: 5: 5)in/12 (12: 13: 13: 13)cm from last set of cast-on sts, ending with a WS row.

Shape overarm seam and shoulders
Bind/cast off 20 (22: 23: 25: 25) sts at beg of next 2 rows, 20 (20: 23: 23: 25) sts at beg of foll 4 rows, 20 sts at beg of next 4 rows, 18 sts at beg of foll 2 rows, and then 12 sts at beg of next 2 rows. 80 (82: 82: 84: 84) sts.

Shape back neck
Next row (RS): Bind/cast off 10 sts, K until there are 14 sts on right needle and turn, leaving rem sts on a holder.
Work each side of neck separately.
Bind/cast off 4 sts at beg of next row.
Bind/cast off rem 10 sts.
With RS facing, rejoin yarn to rem sts, bind/cast off center 32 (34: 34: 36: 36) sts, K to end.
Complete to match first side, reversing shapings.

LEFT FRONT

Cast on 13 (16: 20: 23: 27) sts using size 3 (3¹/₄mm) needles.
Beg with a K row, work in St st as foll:
Work 1 row, ending with a RS row.
Cast on 4 sts at beg of next and foll alt row.
21 (24: 28: 31: 35) sts.
Work 1 row, ending with a RS row.
Inc 1 st at beg of next row and at same edge (front opening edge) of next 4 rows, ending with a WS row.
26 (29: 33: 36: 40) sts.
Inc 1 st at side seam edge of next and foll 10th row, then on foll 8th row, then on foll 6th row **and at same time** inc 1 st at front opening edge of next 5 rows, then on foll 7 alt rows, then on foll 4th row.
43 (46: 50: 53: 57) sts.
Inc 1 st at side seam edge of 4th and 2 foll 4th rows **and at same time** inc 1 st at front opening edge of 2nd and foll 6th row.
48 (51: 55: 58: 62) sts.
Work 1 row, ending with a WS row.
Inc 1 st at side seam edge of next and foll 5 alt rows, then on foll 5 rows **and at same time** inc 1 st at front opening edge on next and foll 8th row, ending with a WS row.
61 (64: 68: 71: 75) sts.
Cast on 3 sts at beg and inc 1 st at end of next row.
65 (68: 72: 75: 79) sts.
Work 1 row, ending with a WS row.
Cast on 3 sts at beg of next and foll alt row, 4 sts at beg of foll 6 alt rows, 6 sts at beg of foll alt row, 8 sts at beg of foll 2 alt rows, 10 sts at beg of foll alt row, 18 sts at beg of foll alt row, and then 18 (18: 21: 21: 21) sts at beg of foll alt row.
163 (166: 173: 176: 180) sts.
Work even/straight until 7 (7: 7: 9: 9) rows less have been worked than on back to start of overarm and shoulder shaping, ending with a RS row.

Shape neck
Bind/cast off 3 (4: 4: 4: 4) sts at beg of next row. 160 (162: 169: 172: 176) sts.
Dec 1 st at neck edge of next 6 rows, then on foll 0 (0: 0: 1: 1) alt row, ending with a WS row.
154 (156: 163: 165: 169) sts.

Shape overarm seam and shoulder
Bind/cast off 20 (22: 23: 25: 25) sts at beg of next row, 20 (20: 23: 23: 25) sts at beg of foll 2 alt rows, 20 sts at beg of foll 2 alt rows, then 18

sts at beg of foll alt row **and at same time** dec 1 st at neck edge of 2nd and foll 2 alt rows, then on foll 4th row. 32 sts.

Work 1 row, ending with a WS row.

Bind/cast off 12 sts at beg of next row, then 10 sts at beg of foll alt row.

Work 1 row.

Bind/cast off rem 10 sts.

RIGHT FRONT

Cast on 13 (16: 20: 23: 27) sts using size 3 (3¼mm) needles.

Beg with a K row, work in St st as foll:

Work 2 rows, ending with a WS row.

Cast on 4 sts at beg of next and foll alt row, ending with a RS row. 21 (24: 28: 31: 35) sts.

Inc 1 st at end of next row and at same edge (front opening edge) of next 4 rows, ending with a WS row. 26 (29: 33: 36: 40) sts.

Inc 1 st at side seam edge of next and foll 10th row, then on foll 8th row, then on foll 6th row **and at same time** inc 1 st at front opening edge of next 5 rows, then on foll 7 alt rows, then on foll 4th row. 43 (46: 50: 53: 57) sts.

Complete to match left front, reversing shapings.

FINISHING

PRESS as described on page 136.

Join both overarm and shoulder seams using backstitch, or mattress stitch if preferred.

Cuffs (both alike)

With RS facing and using size 2 (2¾mm) needles, pick up and knit 65 (65: 69: 69: 69) sts across row-end edge of sleeve sections.

Row 1 (WS): P1, *K1, P1, rep from * to end.

Row 2: K1, *bead 1, K1, rep from * to end.

Row 3: As row 1.

Row 4: K1, *P1, K1, rep from * to end.

Rep last 4 rows once more.

Bind/cast off in rib.

Join side, underarm, and cuff seams using backstitch, or mattress stitch if preferred.

Left front edging

Cast on 9 sts using size 2 (2¾mm) needles.

Row 1 (RS): K2, *P1, K1, rep from * to last st, K1.

Row 2: K1, *P1, K1, rep from * to end.

Row 3: K2, *bead 1, K1, rep from * to last st, K1.

Row 4: As row 2.

These 4 rows form beaded rib patt.

Cont in beaded rib patt until edging fits neatly along left front opening edge, from left side seam to neck shaping, ending after patt row 4 and with a WS row.

Break yarn and leave sts on a holder.

Slip stitch edging in place.

Back and right front edging

Cast on 9 sts using size 2 (2¾mm) needles.

Work in beaded rib patt as given for left front edging until edging fits neatly across back cast-on edge and up right front opening edge, from right side seam to neck shaping, ending after patt row 4 and with a WS row.

Do NOT break yarn.

Slip stitch edging in place.

Neckband

With RS facing and using size 2 (2¾mm) needles, patt across 9 sts of back and right front edging, pick up and knit 26 (27: 27: 29: 29) sts up right side of neck, 41 (43: 43: 45: 45) sts from back, and 26 (27: 27: 29: 29) sts down left side of neck, then patt across 9 sts of left front edging. 111 (115: 115: 121: 121) sts.

Work in beaded rib patt as set by edging sts for 7 rows, ending with a WS row.

Bind/cast off in rib.

Attach hook and eye at neck edge.

47¾ (48½: 50½: 51½: 52½)in [121.5 (123.5: 128.5: 131: 133.5)cm]

16½ (16½: 17: 17: 17)in [42 (42: 43: 43: 43)cm]

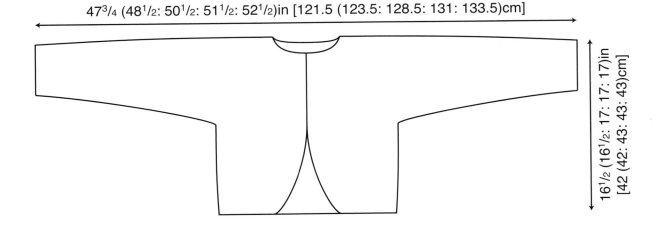

BRIDGET
MARTIN STOREY

This cardigan, knitted up here in black and white, takes us back to winter holidays in the '50s. The playful motifs and concertina-like geometrics are reminders of the paper cutouts children make before Christmas to decorate the classroom windows. The black and white is tempered here by the pink blouse, which softens the look.

BRIDGET
MARTIN STOREY

YARN AND SIZES

	XS	S	M	L	XL	
To fit bust	32	34	36	38	40	in
	81	86	91	97	102	cm

Rowan Yorkshire Tweed 4 ply

A = black (no. 283) or desired MC

	9	10	10	11	12	x 25g

B = off-white (no. 263) or desired CC

	7	7	7	8	8	x 25g

NEEDLES

1 pair size 2 (2³/₄mm) needles
1 pair size 3 (3¹/₄mm) needles

BUTTONS—7 buttons (Rowan 00315)

GAUGE/TENSION

30 sts and 36 rows to 4in/10cm measured over
patterned St st using size 3 (3¹/₄mm) needles.

BACK

Cast on 121 (129: 137: 145: 153) sts using
size 2 (2³/₄mm) needles and yarn A.
Row 1 (RS): K1, *P1, K1, rep from * to end.
Row 2: As row 1.
These 2 rows form seed/moss st.
Work in seed/moss st for 11 rows more, ending
with a RS row.
Row 14 (WS): Seed/moss st 6 (6: 5: 5: 4) sts,
M1, *seed/moss st 12 (13: 14: 15: 16) sts, M1,
rep from * to last 7 (6: 6: 5: 5) sts, seed/moss st
to end. 131 (139: 147: 155: 163) sts.
Change to size 3 (3¹/₄mm) needles.
Starting and ending rows as indicated, using
the **Fair Isle** technique, and **repeating chart
rows 1 to 6 only,** cont in patt from chart, which
is worked entirely in St st beg with a K row,
as foll:
Dec 1 st at each end of 9th and every foll 6th row
to 121 (129: 137: 145: 153) sts, then on every foll
4th row until 113 (121: 129: 137: 145) sts rem.
Work 9 rows, ending with a WS row.
Inc 1 st at each end of next and every foll 6th

row until there are 131 (139: 147: 155: 163)
sts, taking inc sts into patt.
Work even/straight until back measures approx
13¹/₂ (14: 14¹/₄: 14¹/₂: 14¹/₂)in/34 (35: 35: 36:
36)cm, ending after chart row 6 and with a
WS row.
Now working chart rows 7 to 12 **once only** and
then repeating chart rows 13 to 52 **throughout,**
cont as foll:
Work 4 rows, ending with a WS row.
Shape armholes
Keeping patt correct, bind/cast off 6 (7: 7: 8: 8)
sts at beg of next 2 rows.
119 (125: 133: 139: 147) sts.
Dec 1 st at each end of next 5 (5: 7: 7: 9) rows,
then on foll 3 (4: 5: 6: 7) alt rows, then on every
foll 4th row until 99 (103: 105: 109: 111) sts rem.
Work even/straight until armhole measures 8
(8: 8¹/₄: 8¹/₄: 8¹/₂)in/20 (20: 21: 21: 22)cm,
ending with a WS row.
Shape shoulders and back neck
Bind/cast off 9 (9: 9: 10: 10) sts at beg of next 2
rows. 81 (85: 87: 89: 91) sts.
Next row (RS): Bind/cast off 9 (9: 9: 10: 10) sts,
patt until there are 12 (13: 14: 13: 14) sts on right
needle and turn, leaving rem sts on a holder.
Work each side of neck separately.
Bind/cast off 4 sts at beg of next row.
Bind/cast off rem 8 (9: 10: 9: 10) sts.
With RS facing, rejoin yarns to rem sts,
bind/cast off center 39 (41: 41: 43: 43) sts, patt
to end.
Complete to match first side, reversing
shapings.

LEFT FRONT

Cast on 69 (73: 77: 81: 85) sts using size 2
(2³/₄mm) needles and yarn A.
Work in seed/moss st as given for back for 13
rows, ending with a RS row.
Row 14 (WS): Seed/moss st 8 sts and slip
these sts onto a holder, seed/moss st 6 sts, M1,
*seed/moss st 12 (13: 14: 15: 16) sts, M1, rep

from * to last 7 sts, seed/moss st to end.
66 (70: 74: 78: 82) sts.
Change to size 3 (3¹/₄mm) needles.
Starting and ending rows as indicated and
repeating chart rows 1 to 6 only, cont in patt
from chart as foll:
Dec 1 st at beg of 9th and every foll 6th row to
61 (65: 69: 73: 77) sts, then on every foll 4th
row until 57 (61: 65: 69: 73) sts rem.
Work 9 rows, ending with a WS row.
Inc 1 st at beg of next and every foll 6th row
until there are 66 (70: 74: 78: 82) sts, taking inc
sts into patt.
Work even/straight until left front measures
approx 13¹/₂ (14: 14¹/₄: 14¹/₂: 14¹/₂)in/34 (35:
35: 36: 36)cm, ending after chart row 6 and
with a WS row.
Now working chart rows 7 to 12 **once only** and
then repeating chart rows 13 to 52 **throughout,**
cont as foll:
Work 4 rows, ending with a WS row.
Shape armhole
Keeping patt correct, bind/cast off 6 (7: 7: 8: 8)
sts at beg of next row. 60 (63: 67: 70: 74) sts.
Work 1 row.
Dec 1 st at armhole edge of next 5 (5: 7: 7: 9)
rows, then on foll 3 (4: 5: 6: 7) alt rows, then on
every foll 4th row until 50 (52: 53: 55: 56) sts
rem.
Work even/straight until 21 (21: 21: 23: 23)
rows less have been worked than on back to
start of shoulder shaping, ending with a RS row.
Shape neck
Keeping patt correct, bind/cast off 8 (9: 9: 9: 9)
sts at beg of next row. 42 (43: 44: 46: 47) sts.
Dec 1 st at neck edge of next 12 rows, then on
foll 4 (4: 4: 5: 5) alt rows, ending with a WS
row. 26 (27: 28: 29: 30) sts.
Shape shoulder
Bind/cast off 9 (9: 9: 10: 10) sts at beg of next
and foll alt row.
Work 1 row.
Bind/cast off rem 8 (9: 10: 9: 10) sts.

RIGHT FRONT

Cast on 69 (73: 77: 81: 85) sts using size 2
(2³/₄mm) needles and yarn A.

Work in seed/moss st as given for back for 4
rows, ending with a WS row.

Row 5 (RS): Seed/moss st 2 sts, K2tog, yo (to
make a buttonhole), seed/moss st to end.

Work in seed/moss st for 8 rows more, ending
with a RS row.

Row 14 (WS): Seed/moss st 6 sts, M1,
*seed/moss st 12 (13: 14: 15: 16) sts, M1, rep
from * to last 15 sts, seed/moss st to last 8 sts
and turn, leaving rem 8 sts on a holder.
66 (70: 74: 78: 82) sts.

Change to size 3 (3¹/₄mm) needles.

Starting and ending rows as indicated and
repeating chart rows 1 to 6 only, cont in patt
from chart as foll:

Dec 1 st at end of 9th and every foll 6th row to
61 (65: 69: 73: 77) sts, then on every foll 4th
row until 57 (61: 65: 69: 73) sts rem.

Complete to match left front, reversing shapings.

SLEEVES (both alike)

Cast on 63 (63: 65: 67: 67) sts using size 2
(2³/₄mm) needles and yarn A.

Work in seed/moss st as given for back for 13
rows, ending with a RS row.

Row 14 (WS): Seed/moss st 7 (7: 8: 9: 9) sts,
M1, *seed/moss st 16 sts, M1, rep from * to last
8 (8: 9: 10: 10) sts, seed/moss st to end.
67 (67: 69: 71: 71) sts.

Change to size 3 (3¹/₄mm) needles.

Starting and ending rows as indicated and
repeating chart rows 1 to 6 only, cont in patt
from chart as foll:

Inc 1 st at each end of 7th (7th: 5th: 5th: 5th)
and every foll 8th (8th: 8th: 8th: 6th) row to 87
(97: 103: 105: 89) sts, then on every foll 10th
(10th: -: -: 8th) row until there are 97 (99: -: -:
109) sts, taking inc sts into patt.

Work even/straight until sleeve measures approx
17 (17: 17¹/₂: 17¹/₂: 17¹/₂)in/43 (43: 44: 44:

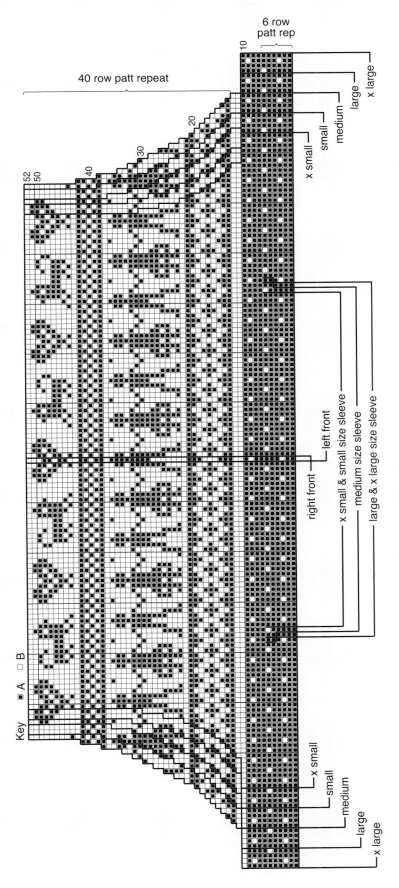

33

44)cm, ending after chart row 6 and with a WS row.

Now working chart rows 7 to 12 **once only** and then repeating chart rows 13 to 52 **throughout**, cont as foll:

Work 4 rows, ending with a WS row.

Shape sleeve cap

Keeping patt correct, bind/cast off 6 (7: 7: 8: 8) sts at beg of next 2 rows. 85 (85: 89: 89: 93) sts.

Dec 1 st at each end of next 5 rows, then on foll 4 alt rows, then on every foll 4th row until 57 (57: 61: 61: 65) sts rem.

Work 1 row, ending with a WS row.

Dec 1 st at each end of next and every foll alt row to 45 sts, then on foll 7 rows, ending with a WS row.

Bind/cast off rem 31 sts.

FINISHING

PRESS as described on page 136.

Join both shoulder seams using backstitch, or mattress stitch if preferred.

Button band

Slip 8 sts left on left front holder onto size 2 (2³/₄mm) needles and rejoin yarn A with RS facing.

Cont in seed/moss st as set until button band, when slightly stretched, fits up left front opening edge to neck shaping, ending with a WS row.

Break yarn and leave sts on a holder.

Mark positions for 7 buttons on this band—first level with buttonhole already worked in right front, last just above neck shaping and rem 5 buttons evenly spaced between.

Buttonhole band

Slip 8 sts left on right front holder onto size 2 (2³/₄mm) needles and rejoin yarn A with WS facing.

Cont in seed/moss st as set until buttonhole band, when slightly stretched, fits up right front opening edge to neck shaping, ending with a WS row and with the addition of 5 buttonholes more worked to correspond with positions

marked for buttons on left front as foll:

Buttonhole row (RS): K1, P1, K2tog, yo, (K1, P1) twice.

When band is complete, do NOT break yarn.

Slip stitch bands in place.

Neckband

With RS facing, using size 2 (2³/₄mm) needles and yarn A, seed/moss st 8 sts of buttonhole band, pick up and knit 30 (31: 31: 33: 33) sts up right side of neck, 47 (49: 49: 51: 51) sts from back, and 30 (31: 31: 33: 33) sts down

left side of neck, then seed/moss st 8 sts of button band. 123 (127: 127: 133: 133) sts.

Work in seed/moss st as set by bands for 1 row, ending with a WS row.

Row 2 (RS): K1, P1, K2tog, yo, seed/moss st to end.

Work in seed/moss st for 2 rows more, ending with a RS row.

Bind/cast off in seed/moss st (on WS).

See page 136 for finishing instructions, setting in sleeves using the set-in method.

17 (18¹/₂: 19¹/₂: 20¹/₂: 21¹/₂)in
[43.5 (46.5: 49: 51.5: 54.5)cm]

22 (22¹/₂: 23: 23¹/₄: 23¹/₂)in
[56 (57: 58: 59: 60)cm]

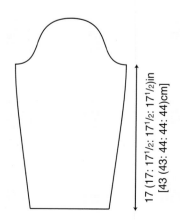

17 (17: 17¹/₂: 17¹/₂: 17¹/₂)in
[43 (43: 44: 44: 44)cm]

CLARK
KIM HARGREAVES

The big turtleneck and the cozy look of this sweater give it a true '50s and '60s feel with the smoldering mood of French film stars. It's a look encapsulated by the singer Jean Paul Belmondo. The seamed effect, marking the transition between the body and the ribbing, is a clever finishing touch.

YARN AND SIZES

	S	M	L	XL	XXL	
To fit chest	38	40	42	44	46	in
	97	102	107	112	117	cm

Rowan Yorkshire Tweed DK

	13	13	14	14	15	x 50g

Use off-white (no. 352) or desired color

NEEDLES

1 pair size 5 (3³/₄mm) needles

1 pair size 6 (4mm) needles

Size 5 (3³/₄mm) circular needle

Size 6 (4mm) circular needle

GAUGE/TENSION

20 sts and 28 rows to 4in/10cm measured over
St st using size 6 (4mm) needles.

BACK

Lower section

Cast on 113 (117: 123: 127: 133) sts using
size 5 (3³/₄mm) needles.

Row 1 (RS): P0 (2: 0: 2: 0), *K3, P2, rep from
* to last 3 (0: 3: 0: 3) sts, K3 (0: 3: 0: 3).

Row 2: K0 (2: 0: 2: 0), *P3, K2, rep from * to
last 3 (0: 3: 0: 3) sts, P3 (0: 3: 0: 3).

These 2 rows form rib.

Cont in rib for 22 rows more, ending with a
WS row. Bind/cast off in rib.

Main section

With WS facing (so that ridge is formed on RS
of work) and using size 6 (4mm) needles, pick
up and knit 113 (117: 123: 127: 133) sts across
bound-off/cast-off edge of lower section.

Beg with a K row, cont in St st until back
measures 15¹/₂ (15³/₄: 16¹/₄: 16¹/₂: 17)in/40 (40:
41: 41: 42)cm from cast-on edge of lower
section, ending with a WS row.

Shape armholes

Bind/cast off 4 sts at beg of next 2 rows.
105 (109: 115: 119: 125) sts.

Next row (RS): K2, K3tog, K to last 5 sts,
K3tog tbl, K2.

Next row: Purl.

Rep last 2 rows twice more.

93 (97: 103: 107: 113) sts.

Work even/straight until armhole measures 8 (8¼: 8¼: 8½: 8½)in/20 (21: 21: 22: 22)cm, ending with a WS row.**

Cont in ridge patt as foll:

Row 1 (RS): Purl.

Rows 2 and 3: Knit.

Row 4: Purl.

These 4 rows form ridge patt.

Work in ridge patt for 6 rows more, ending with a WS row.

Shape back neck

Next row (RS): Patt 29 (30: 33: 34: 36) sts and turn, leaving rem sts on a holder.

Work each side of neck separately.

Bind/cast off 4 sts at beg of next row.

Shape shoulder

Leave rem 25 (26: 29: 30: 32) sts on a holder.

With RS facing, rejoin yarn to rem sts, bind/cast off center 35 (37: 37: 39: 41) sts, patt to end.

Complete to match first side, reversing shapings.

FRONT

Work as given for back to **, ending with a WS row. Beg with row 1, now work in ridge patt as given for back and cont as foll:

Shape neck

Next row (RS): Patt 30 (31: 34: 35: 37) sts and turn, leaving rem sts on a holder.

Work each side of neck separately.

Dec 1 st at neck edge on next 4 rows, then on foll alt row.

25 (26: 29: 30: 32) sts.

Work 5 rows, ending with a WS row.

Shape shoulder

Leave rem 25 (26: 29: 30: 32) sts on a holder.

With RS facing, rejoin yarn to rem sts, bind/cast off center 33 (35: 35: 37: 39) sts, patt to end.

Complete to match first side, reversing shapings.

SLEEVES (both alike)

Lower section

Cast on 63 (63: 65: 67: 67) sts using size 5 (3¾mm) needles.

Row 1 (RS): P0 (0: 1: 2: 2), *K3, P2, rep from * to last 3 (3: 4: 5: 5) sts, K3, P0 (0: 1: 2: 2).

Row 2: K0 (0: 1: 2: 2), *P3, K2, rep from * to last 3 (3: 4: 5: 5) sts, P3, K0 (0: 1: 2: 2).

These 2 rows form rib.

Cont in rib for 30 rows more, ending with a WS row. Bind/cast off in rib.

Main section

With WS facing (so that ridge is formed on RS of work) and using size 6 (4mm) needles, pick up and knit 63 (63: 65: 67: 67) sts across bound-off/cast-off edge of lower section.

Beg with a K row, cont in St st as foll:

Work 2 rows, ending with a WS row.

Next row (RS): K2, M1, K to last 2 sts, M1, K2.

Working all increases as set by last row, inc 1 st at each end of every foll 6th row to 91 (85: 91: 93: 93) sts, then on every foll 4th row until there are 101 (105: 105: 109: 109) sts.

Work even/straight until sleeve measures 20½ (21: 21: 21½: 21½)in/52 (53: 53: 54: 54)cm from cast-on edge of lower section, ending with a WS row.

Shape top of sleeve

Bind/cast off 4 sts at beg of next 2 rows.

93 (97: 97: 101: 101) sts.

Next row (RS): K2, K3tog, K to last 5 sts, K3tog tbl, K2.

Work 3 rows.

Rep last 4 rows twice more.

Bind/cast off rem 81 (85: 85: 89: 89) sts.

FINISHING

PRESS as described on page 136.

Join shoulder seams as foll: holding back and front WS together and working with front toward you, bind/cast off sts of each shoulder edge together, taking one st from front together with one st from back.

Collar

With RS facing and using size 5 (3¾mm) circular needle, starting and ending at left shoulder seam, pick up and knit 13 sts down left side of neck, 32 (35: 35: 37: 39) sts from front, 13 sts up right side of neck, then 42 (44: 44: 47: 50) sts from back.

100 (105: 105: 110: 115) sts.

Round 1 (RS): *K2, P3, rep from * to end.

This round forms rib.

Cont in rib until collar measures 3¼in/8cm.

Change to size 6 (4mm) circular needle.

Cont in rib until collar measures 8in/20cm.

Bind/cast off in rib.

See page 136 for finishing instructions, setting in sleeves using the shallow set-in method.

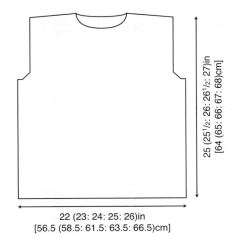

22 (23: 24: 25: 26)in
[56.5 (58.5: 61.5: 63.5: 66.5)cm]

25 (25½: 26: 26½: 27)in
[64 (65: 66: 67: 68)cm]

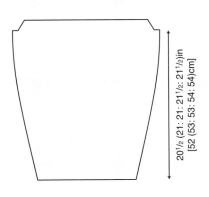

20½ (21: 21: 21½: 21½)in
[52 (53: 53: 54: 54)cm]

AIMEE
KIM HARGREAVES

This pullover is fine and airy. It is knitted loose
enough to show glimpses of the fabric underneath,
creating a layered effect that's enhanced by the bands.
The smooth floral cotton dress perfectly sets off the hazy
surface of the mohair knitting, echoing the autumnal
light filtering through the ancient trees.

AIMEE
KIM HARGREAVES

YARN AND SIZES

	XS	S	M	L	XL	
To fit bust	32	34	36	38	40	in
	81	86	91	97	102	cm

Rowan Kid Silk Haze

	4	4	4	5	5	x 25g

Use fuchsia (no. 583) or desired color

NEEDLES

1 pair size 2 (3mm) needles
1 pair size 3 (3¼mm) needles
1 pair size 5 (3¾mm) needles
1 pair size 7 (4½mm) needles

RIBBON—2½yd/2.3m of 1½in/3.5cm wide ribbon

GAUGE/TENSION

20 sts and 20 rows to 4in/10cm measured over pattern using a combination of size 5 (3¾mm) and TWO STRANDS of yarn held tog, and size 7 (4½mm) needles and ONE STRAND of yarn.

BACK

Cast on 82 (86: 92: 96: 102) sts using size 3 (3¼mm) needles and TWO STRANDS of yarn.
Beg with a K row, work in St st for 10 rows, ending with a WS row.
Change to size 5 (3¾mm) needles.
Row 11 (fold line row) (RS): K1, *skp, yo, rep from * to last st, K1.**
Beg with a P row, work in St st for 11 rows **and at same time** dec 1 st at each end of 6th and foll 4th row, ending with a WS row.
78 (82: 88: 92: 98) sts.
***Cont in patt as foll:
Change to size 7 (4½mm) needles and ONE STRAND of yarn.
Row 1 (RS): Knit.
Row 2: K1, *yo, skp, rep from * to last st, K1.
Row 3: K2tog, K1, *yo, skp, rep from * to last 3 sts, K1, K2tog.
76 (80: 86: 90: 96) sts.

Rows 4 and 5: K2, *yo, skp, rep from * to last 2 sts, K2.
Row 6: Purl.
Change to size 5 (3¾mm) needles and TWO STRANDS of yarn.
Beg with a K row, work in St st for 6 rows **and at same time** dec 1 st at each end of next and foll 4th row, ending with a WS row.
72 (76: 82: 86: 92) sts.
Last 12 rows form lace stripe and St st patt and start side seam shaping.
Cont in patt, dec 1 st at each end of 3rd row.
70 (74: 80: 84: 90) sts.
Work 9 rows, ending with a WS row.
Inc 1 st at each end of next and every foll 4th row until there are 82 (86: 92: 96: 102) sts, taking inc sts into patt.
Work 7 (9: 9: 11: 11) rows, ending with a WS row. Back should measure 12½ (13: 13: 13¼: 13¼)in/32 (33: 33: 34: 34)cm **from fold line row**.

Shape armholes
Keeping patt correct, bind/cast off 3 (4: 4: 5: 5) sts at beg of next 2 rows.
76 (78: 84: 86: 92) sts.
Dec 1 st at each end of next 5 (5: 7: 7: 9) rows, then on foll 3 alt rows. 60 (62: 64: 66: 68) sts.
Work 9 (7: 5: 3: 1) rows more, ending after patt row 2 and with a WS row.
Now repeating last row **only** (to complete work in lace patt), work even/straight until armhole measures 8 (8: 8¼: 8¼: 8¾)in/20 (20: 21: 21: 22)cm, ending with a WS row.

Shape shoulders and back neck
Bind/cast off 4 (4: 4: 4: 5) sts at beg of next 2 rows.
52 (54: 56: 58: 58) sts.
Next row (RS): Bind/cast off 4 (4: 4: 4: 5) sts, patt until there are 8 (8: 9: 9: 8) sts on right needle and turn, leaving rem sts on a holder.
Work each side of neck separately.
Bind/cast off 4 sts at beg of next row.
Bind/cast off rem 4 (4: 5: 5: 4) sts.

With RS facing, rejoin yarn to rem sts, bind/cast off center 28 (30: 30: 32: 32) sts, patt to end.
Complete to match first side, reversing shapings.

FRONT

Work as given for back to **.
Beg with a P row, work in St st for 1 row, ending with a WS row.
Divide for ribbon opening
Next row (RS): K40 (42: 45: 47: 50) and slip these sts onto a holder, bind/cast off 2 sts, K to end.
Work 7 rows on this last set of 40 (42: 45: 47: 50) sts, dec 1 st at end of 4th of these rows and ending with a WS row.
39 (41: 44: 46: 49) sts.
Break yarn and leave sts on another holder.
With **WS** facing, rejoin yarn to 40 (42: 45: 47: 50) sts left on first holder, P to end.
Work 6 rows on these sts, dec 1 st at beg of 3rd of these rows and ending with a WS row.
39 (41: 44: 46: 49) sts.
Join sections
Next row (RS): K2tog, K rem 37 (39: 42: 44: 47) sts, turn and cast on 2 sts, turn and K across first 37 (39: 42: 44: 47) sts left on holder, K2tog.
78 (82: 88: 92: 98) sts.
Work 1 row, ending with a WS row.
Work as given for back from *** until 6 (6: 6: 8: 8) rows less have been worked than on back to start of shoulder shaping, ending with a WS row.
Shape front neck
Next row (RS): Patt 17 (17: 18: 19: 20) sts and turn, leaving rem sts on a holder.
Work each side of neck separately.
Dec 1 st at neck edge of next 4 rows, then on foll 0 (0: 0: 1: 1) alt row.
13 (13: 14: 14: 15) sts.
Work 1 row, ending with a WS row.

Shape shoulder

Bind/cast off 4 (4: 4: 4: 5) sts at beg of next and foll alt row **and at same time** dec 1 st at neck edge of next row.

Work 1 row.

Bind/cast off rem 4 (4: 5: 5: 4) sts.

With RS facing, rejoin yarn to rem sts, bind/cast off center 26 (28: 28: 28: 28) sts, patt to end.

Complete to match first side, reversing shapings.

SLEEVES (both alike)

Cast on 46 (46: 48: 50: 50) sts using size 3 (3¼mm) needles and TWO STRANDS of yarn.

Work in garter st (K every row) for 4 rows, ending with a WS row.

Change to size 5 (3¾mm) needles.

Beg with a K row, work in St st for 4 rows, ending with a WS row.

Cont in patt as foll:

Change to size 7 (4½mm) needles and ONE STRAND of yarn.

Row 1 (RS): Knit.

Rows 2 to 5: K1, *yo, skp, rep from * to last st, K1.

Row 6: Purl.

Change to size 5 (3¾mm) needles and TWO STRANDS of yarn.

Beg with a K row, work in St st for 6 rows, inc 1 st at each end of first of these rows and ending with a WS row. 48 (48: 50: 52: 52) sts.

Last 12 rows form lace stripe and St st patt and start sleeve shaping.

Cont in patt, shaping sides by inc 1 st at each end of 7th (5th: 5th: 5th: 3rd) and every foll 12th (10th: 10th: 10th: 8th) row to 54 (56: 56: 58: 56) sts, then on every foll 14th (12th: 12th: 12th: 10th) row until there are 58 (60: 62: 64: 66) sts, taking inc sts into patt.

Work even/straight until sleeve measures 17 (17: 17½: 17½: 17½)in/43 (43: 44: 44: 44)cm, ending with a WS row.

Shape sleeve cap

Keeping patt correct, bind/cast off 3 (4: 4: 5: 5) sts at beg of next 2 rows.

52 (52: 54: 54: 56) sts.

Dec 1 st at each end of next 3 rows, then on foll 2 alt rows, then on every foll 4th row until 36 (36: 38: 38: 40) sts rem.

Work 1 row, ending with a WS row.

Dec 1 st at each end of next and every foll alt row to 32 sts, then on foll row, ending with a WS row. 30 sts.

Bind/cast off 4 sts at beg of next 2 rows.

Bind/cast off rem 22 sts.

FINISHING

PRESS as described on page 136.

Join right shoulder seam using backstitch, or mattress stitch if preferred.

Neckband

With RS facing, using size 2 (3mm) needles and ONE STRAND of yarn, pick up and knit 10 (10: 10: 12: 12) sts down left side of neck, 26 (28: 28: 28: 28) sts from front, 10 (10: 10: 12: 12) sts up right side of neck, then 36 (38: 38: 40: 40) sts from back.

82 (86: 86: 92: 92) sts.

Beg with a K row, work in rev St st for 4 rows, ending with a RS row.

Bind/cast off **very loosely** knitwise (on WS).

See page 136 for finishing instructions, setting in sleeves using the set-in method.

Fold first 10 rows to inside around lower edge of back and front and slip stitch in place.

Thread ribbon through this channel.

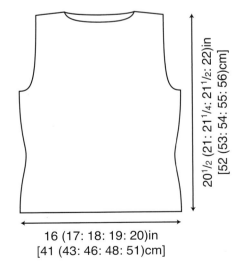

16 (17: 18: 19: 20)in
[41 (43: 46: 48: 51)cm]

20½ (21: 21¼: 21½: 22)in
[52 (53: 54: 55: 56)cm]

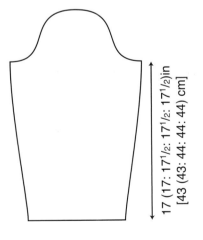

17 (17: 17½: 17½: 17½)in
[43 (43: 44: 44: 44) cm]

ELISE

KIM HARGREAVES

This design, with its low neckline, has a glamorous, even risqué look. The diagonal line is softened by the ruffled edge. The textured handle of the tweed is complemented here by the smooth fabric of the skirt, which continues the figure-hugging line. The side fastening gives a chance to use an eye-catching brooch of your own choice.

YARN AND SIZES

	XS	S	M	L	XL	
To fit bust	32	34	36	38	40	in
	81	86	91	97	102	cm

Rowan Felted Tweed

| | 6 | 7 | 7 | 8 | 8 | x 50g |

Use plum (no. 148) or desired color

NEEDLES

1 pair size 3 (3¹/4mm) needles

1 pair size 5 (3³/4mm) needles

EXTRAS—1yd/1m of narrow ribbon; and decorative brooch

GAUGE/TENSION

23 sts and 32 rows to 4in/10cm measured over St st using size 5 (3³/4mm) needles.

BACK

Cast on 91 (97: 103: 109: 115) sts using size 3 (3¹/4mm) needles.

Work in garter st (K every row) for 4 rows, ending with a WS row.

Change to size 5 (3³/4mm) needles.

Beg with a K row, work in St st for 8 rows, ending with a WS row.

Next row (RS): K2, K2tog, K to last 4 sts, K2tog tbl, K2.

Working all sides seam decreases as set by last row, cont in St st, dec 1 st at each end of every foll 12th row until 85 (91: 97: 103: 109) sts rem.

Work even/straight until back measures 6¹/2 (6³/4: 6³/4: 7¹/4: 7¹/4)in/16 (17: 17: 18: 18)cm, ending with a WS row.

Next row (RS): K2, M1, K to last 2 sts, M1, K2.

Working all side seam increases as set by last row, inc 1 st at each end of every foll 10th row until there are 97 (103: 109: 115: 121) sts.

Work 17 rows, ending with a WS row. Back should measure 14³/4 (15: 15: 15¹/2: 15¹/2)in/37 (38: 38: 39: 39)cm.

Shape armholes

Bind/cast off 4 (5: 5: 6: 6) sts at beg of next 2 rows.

89 (93: 99: 103: 109) sts.

Dec 1 st at each end of next 3 (3: 5: 5: 7) rows, then on foll 3 (4: 4: 5: 5) alt rows.

77 (79: 81: 83: 85) sts.

Work even/straight until armhole measures 8¼ (8¼: 8½: 8½: 9)in/21 (21: 22: 22: 23)cm, ending with a WS row.

Shape shoulders and back neck

Next row (RS): Bind/cast off 6 sts, K until there are 14 (14: 15: 15: 16) sts on right needle and turn, leaving rem sts on a holder.

Work each side of neck separately.

Dec 1 st at beg of next row.

Bind/cast off 6 sts at beg and dec 1 st at end of next row.

Dec 1 st at beg of next row.

Bind/cast off rem 5 (5: 6: 6: 7) sts.

With RS facing, rejoin yarn to rem sts, bind/cast off center 37 (39: 39: 41: 41) sts, K to end.

Complete to match first side, reversing shapings.

LEFT FRONT

Cast on 79 (82: 85: 88: 91) sts using size 3 (3¼mm) needles.

Work in garter st for 4 rows, ending with a WS row.

Change to size 5 (3¾mm) needles.

Row 5 (RS): Knit.

Row 6: K15, P to end.

Last 2 rows set the sts—front opening edge 15 sts in garter st and rem sts in St st.

Keeping sts correct as set, work 6 rows, ending with a WS row.

Working all sides seam decreases as given for back, dec 1 st at beg of next and every foll 12th row until 76 (79: 82: 85: 88) sts rem.

Work even/straight until 6 rows less have been worked than on back to first side seam inc, ending with a WS row.

Next row (RS): Knit.

Next row: K1, (take yarn around needle and draw loop through st on right needle as though to K a st) 4 times (to create short chain), K14, P to end.

Rep last 2 rows once more.

Next row: Knit.

Next row: K1, (take yarn around needle and draw loop through st on right needle as though to K a st) 4 times (to create short chain), K14, wrap next st (by slipping next st to right needle, taking yarn to opposite side of work between needles and then slipping same st back onto left needle—when working back across sts work the wrapped loop tog with the wrapped st), turn, K15, turn, K1, (take yarn around needle and draw loop through st on right needle as though to K a st) 4 times (to create short chain), K14, P to end.

Last 4 rows set the sts—front opening edge 15 sts as ruffle edging and rem sts in St st.

Shape front slope

Next row (RS): K2, M1, K to last 19 sts, K2tog tbl, K17.

76 (79: 82: 85: 88) sts.

This row sets side seam increases and front slope decreases.

Working all increases and decreases as set by last row, dec 1 st at front slope edge of 2nd and foll 12 (14: 13: 15: 13) alt rows, then on 6 (5: 5: 4: 5) foll 4th rows and at same time inc 1 st at side seam edge on 10th and every foll 10th row.

62 (64: 68: 70: 74) sts.

Dec 1 st at front slope edge only on 4th (4th: 2nd: 2nd: 2nd) and every foll 4th row until 58 (60: 64: 66: 70) sts rem.

Work 1 (1: 3: 3: 3) rows, ending with a WS row. (Left front now matches back to beg of armhole shaping.)

Shape armhole

Keeping sts correct, bind/cast off 4 (5: 5: 6: 6) sts at beg and dec 0 (0: 1: 1: 1) st at front slope edge of next row.

54 (55: 58: 59: 63) sts.

Work 1 row.

Dec 1 st at armhole edge of next 3 (3: 5: 5: 7) rows, then on foll 3 (4: 4: 5: 5) alt rows **and at same time** dec 1 st at front slope edge of next (next: 3rd: 3rd: 3rd) and every foll 4th row.

45 (45: 46: 45: 47) sts.

Dec 1 st at front slope edge only on 4th (2nd: 2nd: 4th: 2nd) and every foll 4th row until 33 (33: 34: 34: 35) sts rem.

Work even/straight until left front matches back to start of shoulder shaping, ending with a WS row.

Shape shoulder

Bind/cast off 6 sts at beg of next and foll alt row, then 5 (5: 6: 6: 7) sts at beg of foll alt row.

16 sts.

Cont as set on these 16 sts until shorter edge measures 3½ (3¾: 3¾: 4: 4)in/9 (9.5: 9.5: 10: 10)cm. Bind/cast off.

RIGHT FRONT

Cast on 79 (82: 85: 88: 91) sts using size 3 (3¼mm) needles.

Rows 1 and 2: Knit.

Row 3 (RS): K1, (take yarn around needle and draw loop through st on right needle as though to K a st) 4 times (to create short chain), K14, wrap next st, turn, K15, turn, K1, (take yarn around needle and draw loop through st on right needle as though to K a st) 4 times (to create short chain), K to end.

Row 4: Knit.

Change to size 5 (3¾mm) needles.

Row 5 (RS): K1, (take yarn around needle and draw loop through st on right needle as though to K a st) 4 times (to create short chain), K to end.

Row 6: P to last 15 sts, K15.

Row 7: K1, (take yarn around needle and draw loop through st on right needle as though to K a st) 4 times (to create short chain), K14, wrap next st, turn, K15, turn, K1, (take yarn around needle and draw loop through st on right needle as though to K a st) 4 times (to create short chain), K to end.

Row 8: As row 6.

Last 4 rows set the sts—front opening edge 15 sts as ruffle edging and rem sts in St st. Keeping sts correct as set, work 4 rows, ending with a WS row.

Working all sides seam decreases as given for back, dec 1 st at end of next and every foll 12th row until 76 (79: 82: 85: 88) sts rem.

Work even/straight until right front measures 6½ (6¾: 6¾: 7¼: 7¼)in/16 (17: 17: 18: 18)cm, ending with a WS row.

Shape front slope

Next row (RS): Patt 15 sts, K2, K2tog, K to last 2 sts, M1, K2.

76 (79: 82: 85: 88) sts.

This row sets front slope decreases.

Complete to match left front, reversing shapings.

SLEEVES (both alike)

Cast on 51 (51: 53: 55: 55) sts using size 3 (3¼mm) needles.

Work in garter st for 4 rows, ending with a WS row.

Change to size 5 (3¾mm) needles.

Beg with a K row, work in St st for 6 rows, ending with a WS row.

Next row (RS): K2, M1, K to last 2 sts, M1, K2.

Working all increases as set by last row, inc 1 st at each end of every foll 8th (8th: 8th: 8th: 6th) row to 67 (77: 77: 79: 63) sts, then on every foll 10th (-: 10th: 10th: 8th) row until there are 75 (-: 79: 81: 83) sts.

Work even/straight until sleeve measures 15 (15: 15½: 15½: 15½)in/38 (38: 39: 39: 39)cm, ending with a WS row.

Shape sleeve cap

Bind/cast off 4 (5: 5: 6: 6) sts at beg of next 2 rows. 67 (67: 69: 69: 71) sts.

Dec 1 st at each end of next 5 rows, then on

foll 2 alt rows, then on every foll 4th row until 39 (39: 41: 41: 43) sts rem.

Work 1 row, ending with a WS row.

Dec 1 st at each end of next and every foll alt row to 35 sts, then on foll 7 rows, ending with a WS row.

Bind/cast off rem 21 sts.

FINISHING

PRESS as described on page 136.

Join both shoulder seams using backstitch, or mattress stitch if preferred. Join bound-off/cast-off ends of ruffle strips, then sew shorter edge to back neck, easing in fullness.

Cuffs (both alike)

Cast on 16 sts using size 5 (3¾mm) needles.

Rows 1 and 2: Knit.

Row 3 (RS): K1, (take yarn around needle and draw loop through st on right needle as though to K a st) 4 times (to create short chain), K14, wrap next st, turn, K15, turn, K1, (take yarn around needle and draw loop through st on right needle as though to K a st) 4 times (to create short chain), K to end.

Row 4: Knit.

Row 5: K1, (take yarn around needle and draw loop through st on right needle as though to K a st) 4 times (to create short chain), K to end.

Row 6: Knit.

Last 4 rows form patt.

Cont in patt until shorter edge of cuff fits along cast-on edge of sleeve, ending with a WS row. Bind/cast off.

Sew cuffs to lower edges of sleeves.

See page 136 for finishing instructions, setting in sleeves using the set-in method.

Cut ribbon into two equal lengths and attach one length to inside of left front opening edge, 16 sts on from actual edge and level with start of front slope shaping. Attach other length to inside of right side seam, level with first length. Tie ribbons together to hold left front in place, and fasten right front with a decorative brooch.

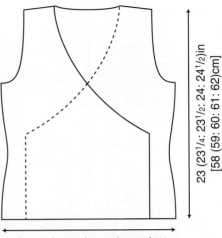

23 (23¼: 23½: 24: 24½)in [58 (59: 60: 61: 62)cm]

16½ (17½: 18½: 19½: 20½)in [42 (45: 47.5: 50: 52.5)cm]

15 (15: 15½: 15½: 15½)in [38 (38: 39: 39: 39)cm]

TYROLEAN
SARAH DALLAS

Waist-length, figure-hugging cardigans were hugely
popular in the 1940s, often knitted in sugar sweet
colors and complex patterns. This version, knitted in
rich dark colors and brightened by rows of embroidered
flowers, is the epitome of sophisticated chic, when
teamed with a classic pencil skirt. The hat and small
Gladstone bag complete the look.

YARN AND SIZES

	XS	S	M	L	XL	
To fit bust	32	34	36	38	40	in
	81	86	91	97	102	cm

Rowan Yorkshire Tweed DK

A = medium brown (no. 355) or desired MC

	9	10	10	11	11	x 50g

B = rose (no. 350) or desired 1st CC

	1	1	1	1	1	x 50g

C = medium green (no. 349) or desired 2nd CC

	1	1	1	1	1	x 50g

D = light green (no. 348) or desired 3rd CC

	1	1	1	1	1	x 50g

NEEDLES

1 pair size 3 (3¼mm) needles
1 pair size 6 (4mm) needles

BUTTONS—7 buttons (Rowan 00320)

GAUGE/TENSION

20 sts and 28 rows to 4in/10cm measured over St st using size 6 (4mm) needles.

SPECIAL ABBREVIATIONS

MB (make bobble) = K into front, back, front, back, and front again of next st, turn, P5, turn, sl 2, K3tog, pass 2 slipped sts over.

BACK

Cast on 82 (86: 90: 94: 102) sts using size 3 (3¼mm) needles and yarn B.
Break off yarn B and join in yarn A.
Row 1 (RS): K2, *P2, K2, rep from * to end.
Row 2: P2, *K2, P2, rep from * to end.
These 2 rows form rib.
Work in rib for 2in/5cm, dec (dec: inc: inc: dec) 1 st at end of last row and ending with a WS row. 81 (85: 91: 95: 101) sts.
Change to size 6 (4mm) needles.
Beg with a K row, cont in St st, shaping side seams by inc 1 st at each end of 3rd and every foll 12th row until there are 91 (95: 101: 105: 111) sts.

Work even/straight until back measures 11¾ (12: 12¼: 12¾: 12¾)in/30 (31: 31: 32: 32)cm, ending with a WS row.

Shape armholes

Bind/cast off 5 (6: 6: 7: 7) sts at beg of next 2 rows. 81 (83: 89: 91: 97) sts.
Dec 1 st at each end of next 5 (5: 7: 7: 9) rows, then on foll 2 alt rows, then on foll 4th row. 65 (67: 69: 71: 73) sts.
Work even/straight until armhole measures 7½ (7½: 7¾: 7¾: 8¼)in/19 (19: 20: 20: 21)cm, ending with a WS row.

Shape shoulders and back neck

Bind/cast off 6 sts at beg of next 2 rows. 53 (55: 57: 59: 61) sts.
Next row (RS): Bind/cast off 6 sts, K until there are 9 (9: 10: 10: 11) sts on right needle and turn, leaving rem sts on a holder.
Work each side of neck separately.
Bind/cast off 4 sts at beg of next row.
Bind/cast off rem 5 (5: 6: 6: 7) sts.
With RS facing, rejoin yarn to rem sts, bind/cast off center 23 (25: 25: 27: 27) sts, K to end.
Complete to match first side, reversing shapings.

LEFT FRONT

Cast on 43 (43: 47: 47: 51) sts using size 3 (3¼mm) needles and yarn B.
Break off yarn B and join in yarn A.
Row 1 (RS): *K2, P2, rep from * to last 3 sts, K3.
Row 2: K1, P2, *K2, P2, rep from * to end.
These 2 rows form rib.
Work in rib for 2in/5cm, dec (-: dec: inc: -) 2 (-: 1: 1: -) sts across last row and ending with a WS row.
41 (43: 46: 48: 51) sts.
Change to size 6 (4mm) needles.
Row 1 (RS): K to last 29 sts, MB, K5, MB, K9, MB, K5, MB, K6.
Row 2: Purl.
Row 3: Inc in first st, K to last 26 sts, MB, K15, MB, K9. 42 (44: 47: 49: 52) sts.

Row 4: Purl.
These 4 rows form patt and start side seam shaping.
Cont in patt, shaping side seam by inc 1 st at beg of 11th and every foll 12th row until there are 46 (48: 51: 53: 56) sts.
Work even/straight until left front matches back to beg of armhole shaping, ending with a WS row.

Shape armhole

Keeping patt correct, bind/cast off 5 (6: 6: 7: 7) sts at beg of next row. 41 (42: 45: 46: 49) sts.
Work 1 row.
Dec 1 st at armhole edge of next 5 (5: 7: 7: 9) rows, then on foll 2 alt rows, then on foll 4th row. 33 (34: 35: 36: 37) sts.
Work even/straight until 17 (17: 17: 19: 19) rows less have been worked than on back to start of shoulder shaping, ending with a RS row.

Shape neck

Keeping patt correct, bind/cast off 8 (9: 9: 9: 9) sts at beg of next row. 25 (25: 26: 27: 28) sts.
Dec 1 st at neck edge on next 5 rows, then on foll 2 (2: 2: 3: 3) alt rows, then on foll 4th row. 17 (17: 18: 18: 19) sts.
Work 3 rows, ending with a WS row.

Shape shoulder

Bind/cast off 6 sts at beg of next and foll alt row.
Work 1 row.
Bind/cast off rem 5 (5: 6: 6: 7) sts.

RIGHT FRONT

Cast on 43 (43: 47: 47: 51) sts using size 3 (3¼mm) needles and yarn B.
Break off yarn B and join in yarn A.
Row 1 (RS): K3, *P2, K2, rep from * to end.
Row 2: P2, *K2, P2, rep from * to last st, K1.
These 2 rows form rib.
Work in rib for 2in/5cm, dec (-: dec: inc: -) 2 (-: 1: 1: -) sts across last row and ending with a WS row.
41 (43: 46: 48: 51) sts.
Change to size 6 (4mm) needles.

Row 1 (RS): K6, MB, K5, MB, K9, MB, K5, MB, K to end.

Row 2: Purl.

Row 3: K9, MB, K15, MB, K to last st, inc in last st. 42 (44: 47: 49: 52) sts.

Row 4: Purl.

These 4 rows form patt and start side seam shaping. Cont in patt, shaping side seam by inc 1 st at end of 11th and every foll 12th row until there are 46 (48: 51: 53: 56) sts.

Complete to match left front, reversing shapings.

SLEEVES (both alike)

Cast on 46 (46: 50: 50: 50) sts using size 3 (3¹/₄mm) needles and yarn B.

Break off yarn B and join in yarn A.

Work in rib as given for back for 2in/5cm, inc (inc: dec: inc: inc) 1 st at end of last row and ending with a WS row. 47 (47: 49: 51: 51) sts. Change to size 6 (4mm) needles.

Row 1 (RS): K15 (15: 16: 17: 17), MB, K15, MB, K to end.

Row 2: Purl.

Row 3: Inc in first st, K11 (11: 12: 13: 13), MB, K5, MB, K9, MB, K5, MB, K to last st, inc in last st. 49 (49: 51: 53: 53) sts.

Row 4: Purl.

These 4 rows form patt and start sleeve shaping. Cont in patt, inc 1 st at each end of 9th (9th: 9th: 9th: 7th) and every foll 12th (10th: 10th: 10th: 8th) row to 65 (63: 63: 65: 57) sts, then on every foll - (12th: 12th: 12th: 10th) row until there are - (67: 69: 71: 73) sts, taking inc sts into St st.

Work even/straight until sleeve measures 17¹/₂ (17¹/₂: 18: 18: 18)in/45 (45: 46: 46: 46)cm, ending with a WS row.

Shape sleeve cap

Keeping patt correct, bind/cast off 5 (6: 6: 7: 7) sts at beg of next 2 rows. 55 (55: 57: 57: 59) sts. Dec 1 st at each end of next 5 rows, then on foll 2 alt rows, then on every foll 4th row until 33 (33: 35: 35: 37) sts rem.

Work 1 row, ending with a WS row.

Dec 1 st at each end of next and every foll alt row to 25 sts, then on foll 3 rows, ending with a WS row. Bind/cast off rem 19 sts.

FINISHING

PRESS as described on page 136.

Join both shoulder seams using backstitch, or mattress stitch if preferred.

Button band

Cast on 7 sts using size 3 (3¹/₄mm) needles and yarn B.

Break off yarn B and join in yarn A.

Row 1 (RS): K2, P1, K1, P1, K2.

Row 2: K1, (P1, K1) 3 times.

These 2 rows form rib.

Cont in rib until button band, when slightly stretched, fits up left front opening edge from cast-on edge to neck shaping, ending with a WS row.

Break yarn and leave sts on a holder.

Slip stitch band in place.

Mark positions for 7 buttons on this band—first to come 1in/2.5cm up from cast-on edge, last to come just above neck shaping, and rem 5 buttons evenly spaced between.

Buttonhole band

Cast on 7 sts using size 3 (3¹/₄mm) needles and yarn B. Break off yarn B and join in yarn A. Cont in rib as given for button band until buttonhole band, when slightly stretched, fits up right front opening edge from cast-on edge to neck shaping, ending with a WS row and working 6 buttonholes to correspond with positions marked for buttons on left front as foll:

Buttonhole row (RS): K2, P2tog, yo, P1, K2.

When band is complete, do NOT break yarn.

Slip stitch band in place.

Neckband

With RS facing, using size 3 (3¹/₄mm) needles and yarn A, rib across 7 sts of buttonhole band, pick up and knit 26 (27: 27: 29: 29) sts up right side of neck, 31 (33: 33: 35: 35) sts from back,

and 26 (27: 27: 29: 29) sts down left side of neck, then rib across 7 sts of button band. 97 (101: 101: 107: 107) sts.

Cont in rib as set by bands for 1 row.

Row 2 (RS): K2, P2tog, yo, rib to end.

Work in rib for 3 rows more.

Bind/cast off in rib.

Embroidery

Following diagram, embroider flowers, stems and leaves onto fronts and sleeves.

See page 136 for finishing instructions, setting in sleeves using the set-in method.

French Knot

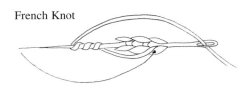

Lazy Daisy

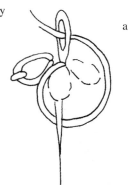

a.

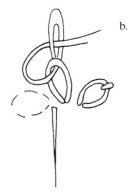

b.

TYROLEAN
SARAH DALLAS

Embroidery Diagram

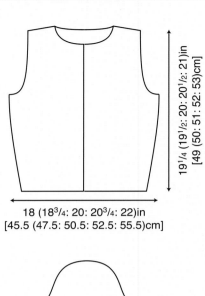

18 (18³⁄₄: 20: 20³⁄₄: 22)in
[45.5 (47.5: 50.5: 52.5: 55.5)cm]

19¹⁄₄ (19¹⁄₂: 20: 20¹⁄₂: 21)in
[49 (50: 51: 52: 53)cm]

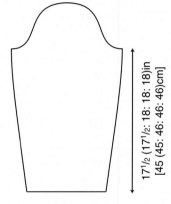

17¹⁄₂ (17¹⁄₂: 18: 18: 18)in
[45 (45: 46: 46: 46)cm]

FAYE
KIM HARGREAVES

More of a wrap than a cardigan, this design is a treat slipped over a period floral dress to keep out the chill fall air. The simple, soft shape makes it ideal to wear for a dinner party, especially with a patterned dress, as in our picture.

FAYE

KIM HARGREAVES

YARN AND SIZES

	XS	S	M	L	XL	
To fit bust	32	34	36	38	40	in
	81	86	91	97	102	cm

Rowan Kid Silk Haze

	8	8	8	9	9	x 25g

Use green-blue (no. 582) or desired color

NEEDLES

1 pair size 3 (3¼mm) needles
1 pair size 5 (3¾mm) needles
2 size 2 (2¾mm) double-pointed needles

GAUGE/TENSION

22 sts and 32 rows to 4in/10cm measured over
pattern using size 5 (3¾mm) needles and
TWO STRANDS of yarn held tog.

BACK

Cast on 95 (101: 107: 113: 119) sts using
size 3 (3¼mm) needles and TWO STRANDS
of yarn.

Row 1 (RS): K1, *P1, K1, rep from * to end.
Row 2: P1, *K1, P1, rep from * to end.
These 2 rows form rib.
Cont in rib for 4¾in/12cm, ending with a
WS row.

Next row (eyelet row) (RS): Rib 2 (5: 2: 5: 2),
*yo, work 2 tog, rib 4, rep from * to last 3 (6:
3: 6: 3) sts, yo, work 2 tog, rib 1 (4: 1: 4: 1).
Cont in rib for 3 rows more, inc 1 st at end of
last row and ending with a WS row.
96 (102: 108: 114: 120) sts.
Change to size 5 (3¾mm) needles.
Row 1 (RS): K0 (1: 0: 1: 0), *K2, yo, skp, rep
from * to last 0 (1: 0: 1: 0) st,
K0 (1: 0: 1: 0).
Row 2: P0 (1: 0: 1: 0), *P2, yo, P2tog, rep
from * to last 0 (1: 0: 1: 0) st, P0 (1: 0: 1: 0).
These 2 rows form patt.
Cont in patt until back measures 14½ (15: 15:
15¼: 15½)in/37 (38: 38: 39: 39)cm, ending
with a WS row.

Shape armholes

Keeping patt correct, bind/cast off 3 (4: 4: 5: 5)
sts at beg of next 2 rows. 90 (94: 100: 104: 110)
sts.
Dec 1 st at each end of next 5 (5: 7: 7: 9) rows,
then on foll 2 (3: 3: 4: 4) alt rows.
76 (78: 80: 82: 84) sts.
Work even/straight until armhole measures 8
(8: 8¼: 8¼: 8½)in/20 (20: 21: 21: 22)cm,
ending with a WS row.

Shape shoulders and back neck

Bind/cast off 7 (7: 8: 8: 8) sts at beg of next 2
rows. 62 (64: 64: 66: 68) sts.
Next row (RS): Bind/cast off 7 (7: 8: 8: 8) sts,
patt until there are 12 (12: 11: 11: 12) sts on
right needle and turn, leaving rem sts on a
holder.
Work each side of neck separately.
Bind/cast off 4 sts at beg of next row.
Bind/cast off rem 8 (8: 7: 7: 8) sts.
With RS facing, rejoin yarn to rem sts,
bind/cast off center 24 (26: 26: 28: 28) sts, patt
to end.
Complete to match first side, reversing shapings.

LEFT FRONT

Cast on 52 (56: 58: 62: 64) sts using size 3
(3¼mm) needles and TWO STRANDS of yarn.
Row 1 (RS): *K1, P1, rep from * to last
2 sts, K2.
Row 2: *K1, P1, rep from * to end.
These 2 rows form rib.
Cont in rib for 4¾in/12cm, ending with a WS
row.
Next row (eyelet row) (RS): Rib 5 (2: 5: 2: 5),
*yo, work 2 tog, rib 4, rep from * to last 5 (6:
5: 6: 5) sts, yo, work 2 tog, rib 3 (4: 3: 4: 3).
Cont in rib for 2 rows more, ending with
a RS row.
Next row (WS): Rib 5 and slip these 5 sts onto
a holder, rib to last 1 (0: 1: 0: 1) st, (inc in last
st) 1 (0: 1: 0: 1) times. 48 (51: 54: 57: 60) sts.
Change to size 5 (3¾mm) needles.

Row 1 (RS): K0 (1: 0: 1: 0), *K2, yo, skp, rep
from * to last 0 (2: 2: 0: 0) sts, K0 (2: 2: 0: 0).
Row 2: P0 (2: 2: 0: 0), *P2, yo, P2tog, rep from
* to last 0 (1: 0: 1: 0) st, P0 (1: 0: 1: 0).
These 2 rows form patt.
Work in patt for 6 rows more, ending with a
WS row.

Shape front slope

Keeping patt correct, dec 1 st at end of next
and every foll 8th row until left front matches
back to beg of armhole shaping, ending with
a WS row.

Shape armhole

Keeping patt correct and still dec 1 st at front
slope edge on every 8th row as set **throughout,**
cont as foll:
Bind/cast off 3 (4: 4: 5: 5) sts at beg of next row.
Work 1 row.
Dec 1 st at armhole edge of next 5 (5: 7: 7: 9)
rows, then on foll 2 (3: 3: 4: 4) alt rows.
Cont to dec at front slope edge on every 8th row
as set until 22 (22: 23: 23: 24) sts rem.
Work even/straight until left front matches back
to start of shoulder shaping, ending with a
WS row.

Shape shoulder

Bind/cast off 7 (7: 8: 8: 8) sts at beg of next and
foll alt row.
Work 1 row. Bind/cast off rem 8 (8: 7: 7: 8) sts.

RIGHT FRONT

Cast on 52 (56: 58: 62: 64) sts using size 3
(3¼mm) needles and TWO STRANDS of yarn.
Row 1 (RS): K2, *P1, K1, rep from * to end.
Row 2: *P1, K1, rep from * to end.
These 2 rows form rib.
Cont in rib for 4¾in/12cm, ending with a
WS row.

Next row (eyelet row) (RS): Rib 3 (4: 3: 4: 3),
work 2 tog tbl, yo, *rib 4, work 2 tog tbl, yo, rep
from * to last 5 (2: 5: 2: 5) sts, rib 5 (2: 5: 2: 5).
Cont in rib for 2 rows more, ending with a
RS row.

Next row (WS): (Inc in first st) 1 (0: 1: 0: 1) times, rib to last 5 sts and turn, leaving last 5 sts on a holder.

48 (51: 54: 57: 60) sts.

Change to size 5 (3³/4mm) needles.

Row 1 (RS): K0 (2: 2: 0: 0), *K2, yo, skp, rep from * to last 0 (1: 0: 1: 0) st, K0 (1: 0: 1: 0).

Row 2: P0 (1: 0: 1: 0), *P2, yo, P2tog, rep from * to last 0 (2: 2: 0: 0) sts, P0 (2: 2: 0: 0).

These 2 rows form patt.

Work in patt for 6 rows more, ending with a WS row.

Shape front slope

Keeping patt correct, dec 1 st at beg of next and every foll 8th row until left front matches back to beg of armhole shaping, ending with a RS row.

Complete to match left front, reversing shapings.

SLEEVES (both alike)

Cast on 57 (57: 59: 61: 61) sts using size 3 (3¹/4mm) needles and TWO STRANDS of yarn.

Work in rib as given for back for 2³/4in/7cm, inc 1 st at end of last row and ending with a WS row.

58 (58: 60: 62: 62) sts.

Change to size 5 (3³/4mm) needles.

Row 1 (RS): K1 (1: 0: 1: 1), *K2, yo, skp, rep from * to last 1 (1: 0: 1: 1) st, K1 (1: 0: 1: 1).

Row 2: P1 (1: 0: 1: 1), *P2, yo, P2tog, rep from * to last 1 (1: 0: 1: 1) st, P1 (1: 0: 1: 1).

These 2 rows form patt.

Cont in patt, shaping sides by inc 1 st at each end of 17th (13th: 13th: 13th: 11th) and every foll 20th (16th: 16th: 16th: 14th) row to 68 (66: 66: 68: 72) sts, then on every foll - (18th: 18th: 18th: 16th) row until there are - (70: 72: 74: 76) sts, taking inc sts into patt.

Work even/straight until sleeve measures 17 (17: 17¹/2: 17¹/2: 17¹/2)in/43 (43: 44: 44: 44)cm, ending with a WS row.

Shape sleeve cap

Keeping patt correct, bind/cast off 3 (4: 4: 5: 5) sts at beg of next 2 rows.

62 (62: 64: 64: 66) sts.

Dec 1 st at each end of next 3 rows, then on foll 2 alt rows, then on every foll 4th row until 40 (40: 42: 42: 44) sts rem.

Work 1 row, ending with a WS row.

Dec 1 st at each end of next and every foll alt row to 36 sts, then on foll 7 rows, ending with a WS row.

Bind/cast off rem 22 sts.

FINISHING

PRESS as described on page 136.

Join both shoulder seams using backstitch, or mattress stitch if preferred.

Left front band

Slip 5 sts from holder onto size 3 (3¹/4mm) needles and rejoin TWO STRANDS of yarn with RS facing.

Cont in rib as set until band, when slightly stretched, fits up left front opening edge and across to center back neck.

Bind/cast off.

Slip stitch band in place.

Right front band

Slip 5 sts from holder onto size 3 (3¹/4mm) needles and rejoin TWO STRANDS of yarn with WS facing.

Cont in rib as set until band, when slightly stretched, fits up right front opening edge and across to center back neck.

Bind/cast off.

Slip stitch band in place, joining ends of bands at center back neck.

Tie

With size 2 (2³/4mm) double-pointed needles and ONE STRAND of yarn, cast on 4 sts.

Row 1 (RS): K4, *without turning work slip these 4 sts to opposite end of needle and bring yarn to opposite end of work pulling it quite tightly across back of these 4 sts, using other

needle K these 4 sts again; rep from * until tie is 51in/130cm long, K4tog, and fasten off.

See page 136 for finishing instructions, setting in sleeves using the set-in method. Thread tie through eyelet row near top of ribbing.

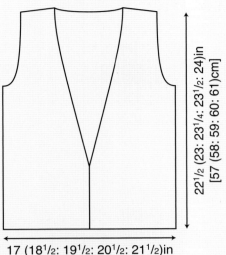

22¹/2 (23: 23¹/4: 23¹/2: 24)in [57 (58: 59: 60: 61)cm]

17 (18¹/2: 19¹/2: 20¹/2: 21¹/2)in [43.5 (46.5: 49: 52: 54.5)cm]

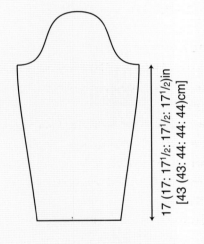

17 (17: 17¹/2: 17¹/2: 17¹/2)in [43 (43: 44: 44: 44)cm]

Mason
KIM HARGREAVES

Rugged enough to look at home on a gardener
pruning the winter vines or a fisherman out on his
fishing boat, the dark hints of color in this roll-neck
supply subtle visual interest. The cabling hints at
ropes and twine.

MASON
KIM HARGREAVES

YARN AND SIZES

	S	M	L	XL	XXL	
To fit chest	38	40	42	44	46	in
	97	102	107	112	117	cm

Rowan Yorkshire Tweed Chunky

	9	10	10	10	11	x 100g

Use charcoal (no. 552) or desired color

NEEDLES

1 pair size 10$\frac{1}{2}$ (7mm) needles
1 pair size 11 (8mm) needles
Cable needle

GAUGE/TENSION

12 sts and 16 rows to 4in/10cm measured over
St st using size 11 (8mm) needles.

SPECIAL ABBREVIATIONS

C10B = slip next 5 sts onto cable needle and
leave at back of work, K5, then K5 from cable
needle.

C10F = slip next 5 sts onto cable needle and
leave at front of work, K5, then K5 from cable
needle.

BACK

Cast on 74 (76: 80: 82: 86) sts using size 10$\frac{1}{2}$
(7mm) needles.
Row 1 (RS): K0 (0: 1: 0: 0), P0 (1: 2: 0: 2),
*K2, P2, rep from * to last 2 (3: 1: 2: 0) sts,
K2 (2: 1: 2: 0), P0 (1: 0: 0: 0).
Row 2: P0 (0: 1: 0: 0), K0 (1: 2: 0: 2), *P2, K2,
rep from * to last 2 (3: 1: 2: 0) sts, P2 (2: 1: 2:
0), K0 (1: 0: 0: 0).
These 2 rows form rib.
Cont in rib for 12 rows more, ending with a
WS row.
Change to size 11 (8mm) needles.
Row 1 (RS): P12 (13: 15: 16: 18), K10, P30,
K10, P to end.
Row 2 and every foll alt row: K12 (13: 15:
16: 18), P10, K30, P10, K to end.
Rows 3, 5, and 7: As row 1.

Row 9: P12 (13: 15: 16: 18), C10B, P30,
C10F, P to end.
Row 11: As row 1.
Row 12: As row 2.
These 12 rows form patt.
Cont in patt until back measures 16$\frac{3}{4}$ (17:
17$\frac{1}{2}$: 17$\frac{1}{4}$: 17$\frac{1}{2}$)in/43 (43: 44: 44: 45)cm,
ending with a WS row.
Shape armholes
Keeping patt correct, bind/cast off 4 sts at beg
of next 2 rows.
66 (68: 72: 74: 78) sts.
Dec 1 st at each end of next 3 (3: 5: 5: 7) rows,
then on foll 3 alt rows.
54 (56: 56: 58: 58) sts.
Work even/straight until armhole measures 8$\frac{3}{4}$
(9: 9: 9$\frac{1}{2}$: 9$\frac{1}{2}$)in/22 (23: 23: 24: 24)cm, ending
with a WS row.
Shape shoulders and back neck
Bind/cast off 5 sts at beg of next 2 rows.
44 (46: 46: 48: 48) sts.
Next row (RS): Bind/cast off 5 sts, patt until
there are 9 sts on right needle and turn, leaving
rem sts on a holder.
Work each side of neck separately.
Bind/cast off 4 sts at beg of next row.
Bind/cast off rem 5 sts.
With RS facing, rejoin yarn to rem sts, cast off
center 16 (18: 18: 20: 20) sts, patt to end.
Complete to match first side, reversing shapings.

FRONT

Work as given for back until 10 (10: 12:
12: 12) rows less have been worked than on
back to start of shoulder shaping, ending
with a WS row.
Shape neck
Next row (RS): Patt 22 (22: 23: 23: 23) sts and
turn, leaving rem sts on a holder.
Work each side of neck separately.
Dec 1 st at neck edge of next 6 rows, then on
foll 1 (1: 2: 2: 2) alt rows. 15 sts.
Work 1 row, ending with a WS row.

Shape shoulder
Bind/cast off 5 sts at beg of next and foll alt row.
Work 1 row.
Bind/cast off rem 5 sts.
With RS facing, rejoin yarn to rem sts,
bind/cast off center 10 (12: 10: 12: 12) sts,
patt to end.
Complete to match first side, reversing shapings.

LEFT SLEEVE

Cast on 40 (40: 40: 42: 42) sts using size 10$\frac{1}{2}$
(7mm) needles.
Row 1 (RS): K1 (1: 1: 2: 2), P2, *K2, P2, rep
from * to last 1 (1: 1: 2: 2) sts, K1 (1: 1: 2: 2).
Row 2: P1 (1: 1: 2: 2), K2, *P2, K2, rep from *
to last 1 (1: 1: 2: 2) sts, P1 (1: 1: 2: 2).
These 2 rows form rib.
Cont in rib for 14 rows more, ending with a
WS row.
Change to size 11 (8mm) needles.
Row 1 (RS): Inc in first st, P14 (14: 14: 15: 15),
K10, P to last st, inc in last st.
42 (42: 42: 44: 44) sts.
Row 2: K16 (16: 16: 17: 17), P10, K to end.
Row 3: P16 (16: 16: 17: 17), K10, P to end.
Rows 4 to 7: As rows 2 and 3, twice.
Row 8: As row 3.
Row 9: Inc in first st, P15 (15: 15: 16: 16),
C10F, P to last st, inc in last st.
44 (44: 44: 46: 46) sts.
Row 10: K17 (17: 17: 18: 18), P10, K to end.
Row 11: P17 (17: 17: 18: 18), K10, P to end.
Row 12: As row 10.
These 12 rows form patt and start sleeve
shaping.
Cont in patt, shaping sides by inc 1 st at each
end of 5th and every foll 8th row to 48 (56: 56:
56: 56) sts, then on every foll 10th (-: -: 10th:
10th) row until there are 54 (-: -: 58: 58) sts,
taking inc sts into rev St st.
Work even/straight until sleeve measures 19$\frac{1}{4}$
(19$\frac{1}{2}$: 19$\frac{1}{2}$: 20: 20)in/49 (50: 50: 51: 51)cm,
ending with a WS row.

Shape sleeve cap

Keeping patt correct, bind/cast off 4 sts at beg of next 2 rows.

46 (48: 48: 50: 50) sts.

Dec 1 st at each end of next 3 rows, then on foll alt row, then on every foll 4th row until 32 (34: 34: 36: 36) sts rem.

Work 1 row, ending with a WS row.

Dec 1 st at each end of next and foll 0 (1: 1: 2: 2) alt rows, then on foll 3 rows, ending with a WS row.

Bind/cast off rem 24 sts.

RIGHT SLEEVE

Work as given for left sleeve, but replacing "C10F" of patt with "C10B".

FINISHING

PRESS as described on page 136.

Join right shoulder seam using backstitch, or mattress stitch if preferred.

Collar

With RS facing and using size 10½ (7mm) needles, pick up and knit 14 (14: 15: 15: 15) sts down left side of neck, 10 (12: 10: 12: 12) sts from front, 14 (14: 15: 15: 15) sts up right side of neck, then 24 (26: 26: 28: 28) sts from back.

62 (66: 66: 70: 70) sts.

Row 1 (WS): P2, *K2, P2, rep from * to end.

Row 2: K2, *P2, K2, rep from * to end.

These 2 rows form rib.

Cont in rib until collar measures 3¼in/8cm.

Change to size 11 (8mm) needles.

Cont in rib until collar measures 8in/20cm.

Bind/cast off in rib.

See page 136 for finishing instructions, setting in sleeves using the set-in method.

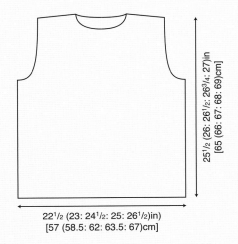

22½ (23: 24½: 25: 26½)in
[57 (58.5: 62: 63.5: 67)cm]

25½ (26: 26½: 26¾: 27)in
[65 (66: 67: 68: 69)cm]

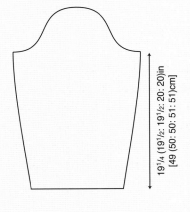

19¼ (19½: 19½: 20: 20)in
[49 (50: 50: 51: 51)cm]

JOLIE

KIM HARGREAVES

There's a touch of homespun quaintness about this low fastening cardigan,
which enhances a curvy figure. The nubbly surface, seen here in a neutral color,
reflects the natural slightly uneven materials of the village street: the crumbly plaster,
the distressed shutters, the cobbles underfoot.

JOLIE
KIM HARGREAVES

YARN AND SIZES

	XS	S	M	L	XL	
To fit bust	32	34	36	38	40	in
	81	86	91	97	102	cm

Rowan Yorkshire Tweed Aran

| | 5 | 5 | 6 | 6 | 7 | x 100g |

Use ecru (no. 417) or desired color

NEEDLES & HOOK

1 pair size 8 (5mm) needles
Size J-10 (6.00mm) crochet hook

BUTTONS—9 buttons (Rowan 00339 or buttons of your choice

GAUGE/TENSION

17 ½ sts and 29 rows to 4in/10cm measured over pattern using size 8 (5mm) needles.

ABBREVIATIONS

sc = single crochet (double crochet in UK)

BACK

Left side panel

Cast on 24 (26: 28: 30: 32) sts using size 8 (5mm) needles.

Starting and ending rows as indicated, working chart rows 1 to 18 **seven times in total,** then working chart rows 19 to 24 **once only** and then repeating chart rows 25 to 38 throughout, cont in patt from chart for body as foll:

Dec 1 st at end of 15th and every foll 6th row to 21 (23: 25: 27: 29) sts, then on every foll 4th row until 19 (21: 23: 25: 27) sts rem.

Work 1 row, ending with a WS row.

Break yarn and leave sts on a holder.

Center panel

Cast on 35 sts using size 8 (5mm) needles.

Starting and ending rows as indicated, cont in patt from chart for body as foll:

Work 36 rows, ending with a WS row.

Break yarn and leave sts on a holder.

Right side panel

Cast on 24 (26: 28: 30: 32) sts using size 8 (5mm) needles. Starting and ending rows as indicated, cont in patt from chart for body as foll:

Dec 1 st at beg of 15th and every foll 6th row to 21 (23: 25: 27: 29) sts, then on every foll 4th row until 19 (21: 23: 25: 27) sts rem.

Work 1 row, ending with a WS row.

Join panels

Next row (RS): Patt to last 4 sts of right side panel, holding WS of center panel against RS of right side panel, patt tog first st of center panel with next st of right side panel, patt tog next 3 sts of center panel with rem 3 sts of right side panel in same way, patt to last 4 sts of center panel, holding WS of center panel against RS of left side panel, patt tog next st of center panel with first st of left side panel, patt tog last 3 sts of center panel with next 3 sts of left side panel in same way, patt to end. 65 (69: 73: 77: 81) sts.

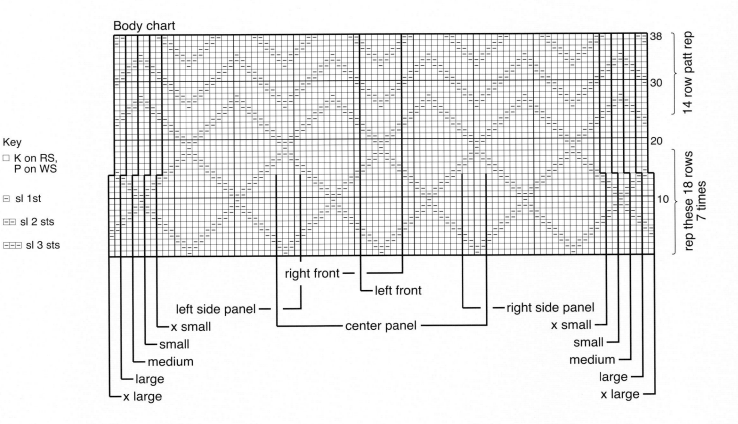

Body chart

Key
☐ K on RS,
 P on WS

⊟ sl 1st

⊟⊟ sl 2 sts

⊟⊟⊟ sl 3 sts

38
30
20
10

14 row patt rep

rep these 18 rows 7 times

right front —
left front —
left side panel —
x small
small
medium
large
x large
center panel —
right side panel —
x small
small
medium
large
x large

Work 1 row.

Dec 1 st at each end of next row.

63 (67: 71: 75: 79) sts.

Work even/straight until back measures 6 (6½: 6¾: 7¼: 7¼)in/16 (17: 17: 18: 18)cm, ending with a WS row.

Inc 1 st at each end of next and every foll 8th row until there are 75 (79: 83: 87: 91) sts, taking inc sts into patt.

Work 13 rows, ending with a WS row. Back should measure 13½ (14: 14¼: 14¾: 14¾)in/35 (36: 36: 37: 37)cm.

Shape armholes

With patt correct, bind/cast off 3 (4: 4: 5: 5) sts at beg of next 2 rows. 69 (71: 75: 77: 81) sts.

Dec 1 st at each end of next 3 rows, then on foll 3 (3: 4: 4: 5) alt rows. 57 (59: 61: 63: 65) sts.

Work even/straight until armhole measures 8 (8: 8¼: 8¼: 8½)in/20 (20: 21: 21: 22)cm, ending with a WS row.

Shape shoulders and back neck

Bind/cast off 5 (5: 6: 6: 6) sts at beg of next 2 rows.

47 (49: 49: 51: 53) sts.

Next row (RS): Bind/cast off 5 (5: 6: 6: 6) sts, patt until there are 10 (10: 9: 9: 10) sts on right needle and turn, leaving rem sts on a holder.

Work each side of neck separately.

Bind/cast off 4 sts at beg of next row.

Bind/cast off rem 6 (6: 5: 5: 6) sts.

With RS facing, rejoin yarn to rem sts, bind/cast off center 17 (19: 19: 21: 21) sts, patt to end.

Complete to match first side, reversing shapings.

LEFT FRONT

Cast on 41 (43: 45: 47: 49) sts using size 8 (5mm) needles.

Starting and ending rows as indicated, cont in patt from chart for body as foll:

Dec 1 st at beg of 15th and every foll 6th row to 38 (40: 42: 44: 46) sts, then on every foll 4th row until 35 (37: 39: 41: 43) sts rem.

Work even/straight until left front measures

6 (6½: 6¾: 7¼: 7¼)in/16 (17: 17: 18: 18)cm, ending with a WS row.

Inc 1 st at beg of next row. 36 (38: 40: 42: 44) sts. Work 7 rows, ending with a WS row.

Shape front slope

Inc 1 st at side seam edge (beg) of next and 4 foll 8th rows **and at same time** dec 1 st at front slope edge (end) of next and 5 foll 4th rows, then on every foll 6th row. 33 (35: 37: 39: 41) sts.

Dec 1 st at front slope edge **only** of 6th and foll 0 (6th: 6th: 6th: 6th) row. 32 (33: 35: 37: 39) sts.

Work 7 (1: 1: 1: 1) rows, ending with a WS row. (Left front now matches back to beg of armhole shaping.)

Shape armholes

Keeping patt correct, bind/cast off 3 (4: 4: 5: 5) sts at beg and dec 1 (0: 0: 0: 0) st at end of next row. 28 (29: 31: 32: 34) sts. Work 1 row.

Dec 1 st at armhole edge of next 3 rows, then on foll 3 (3: 4: 4: 5) alt rows **and at same time** dec 1 st at front slope edge of 7th (3rd: 3rd: 3rd: 3rd) and foll 0 (6th: 6th: 6th: 6th) row. 21 (21: 22: 23: 24) sts.

Dec 1 st at front slope edge **only** on 6th (6th: 6th: 4th: 2nd) and every foll 8th (8th: 8th: 6th: 6th) to 16 (16: 17: 19: 22) sts, then on every foll - (-: -: 8th: 8th) until - (-: -: 17: 18) sts rem.

Work even/straight until left front matches back to start of shoulder shaping, ending with WS row.

Shape shoulder

Bind/cast off 5 (5: 6: 6: 6) sts at beg of next and foll alt row.

Work 1 row. Bind/cast off rem 6 (6: 5: 5: 6) sts.

Mark positions for 3 buttons along left front opening edge—first to come level with row 37, third to come just below start of front slope shaping, and second to come midway between.

RIGHT FRONT

Cast on 41 (43: 45: 47: 49) sts using size 8 (5mm) needles.

Starting and ending rows as indicated, cont in patt from chart for body as foll:

Dec 1 st at end of 15th and every foll 6th row to 38 (40: 42: 44: 46) sts, then on every foll 4th row until 36 (38: 40: 44) sts rem.

Work 1 row, ending with a WS row.

Row 37 (buttonhole row) (RS): Patt 3 sts, bind/cast off 2 sts (to make a buttonhole—cast on 2 sts over these bound-off/cast-off sts on next row), patt to end. Work 1 row.

Dec 1 st at end of next row. 35 (37: 39: 41: 43) sts.

Complete to match left front, reversing shapings and making 2 buttonholes more to correspond with positions marked for buttons.

LEFT SLEEVE

Front panel

Cast on 31 (31: 31: 32: 32) sts using size 8 (5mm) needles.

Starting and ending rows as indicated, working chart rows 1 to 28 **once only,** and then repeating chart rows 29 to 46 throughout, cont in patt from chart for sleeve as foll:

Work 28 rows, ending with a WS row.

Break yarn and leave sts on a holder.

Back panel

Cast on 18 (18: 18: 19: 19) sts using size 8 (5mm) needles.

Starting and ending rows as indicated, cont in patt from chart for sleeve as foll:

Work 28 rows, ending with a WS row.

Join panels

Next row (RS): Patt to last 4 sts of back panel, holding WS of front panel against RS of back panel, patt tog first st of front panel with next st of back panel, patt tog next 3 sts of front panel with rem 3 sts of back panel in same way, patt to end. 45 (45: 45: 47: 47) sts.

**Work 1 row.

Inc 1 st at each end of next and every foll 20th (16th: 14th: 14th: 12th) row until there are 55 (57: 59: 61: 63) sts, taking inc sts into patt.

Work even/straight until sleeve measures 17 (17: 17½: 17½: 17½)in/43 (43: 44: 44: 44)cm, ending with a WS row.

Shape sleeve cap

Keeping patt correct, bind/cast off 3 (4: 4: 5: 5) sts at beg of next 2 rows. 49 (49: 51: 51: 53) sts. Dec 1 st at each end of next 3 rows, then on foll alt row, then on foll 4th row, then on every foll 6th row until 33 (33: 35: 35: 37) sts rem.

Work 3 rows, ending with a WS row.

Dec 1 st at each end of next and every foll alt row to 27 sts, then on foll 3 rows, ending with a WS row.

Bind/cast off rem 21 sts.

RIGHT SLEEVE

Back panel

Cast on 18 (18: 18: 19: 19) sts using size 8 (5mm) needles.

Starting and ending rows as indicated, cont in patt from chart for sleeve as foll:

Work 28 rows, ending with a WS row.

Break yarn and leave sts on a holder.

Front panel

Cast on 31 (31: 31: 32: 32) sts using size 8 (5mm) needles.

Starting and ending rows as indicated, cont in patt from chart for sleeve as foll:

Work 28 rows, ending with a WS row.

Join panels

Next row (RS): Patt to last 4 sts of front panel, holding WS of front panel against RS of back panel, patt tog next st of front panel with first st of back panel, patt tog rem 3 sts of front panel with next 3 sts of back panel in same way, patt to end. 45 (45: 45: 47: 47) sts.

Complete as given for left sleeve from **.

FINISHING

PRESS as described on page 136.

Join both shoulder seams using backstitch.

See page 136 for finishing instructions, setting in sleeves using the set-in method.

Edging

Using size J-10 (6.00mm) crochet hook and starting where right back panel joins center panel, work 1 row of sc evenly down right back panel row-end edge, across cast-on edge to front opening edge, up front opening edge and front slope, across back neck, down left front slope and opening edge, across cast-on edge to back vent, then up row-end edge of left back panel to where left back panel joins center panel, working 2sc in corners and ensuring edging lays flat, do NOT turn. Now work 1 row of crab st (sc worked from left to right, instead of right to left).

Fasten off.

In same way, work edging along row-end and cast-on edges of back center panel, then along sleeve cast-on and row-end edges of panels.

Using photograph as a guide, attach 3 buttons to each cuff, attaching buttons through both layers.

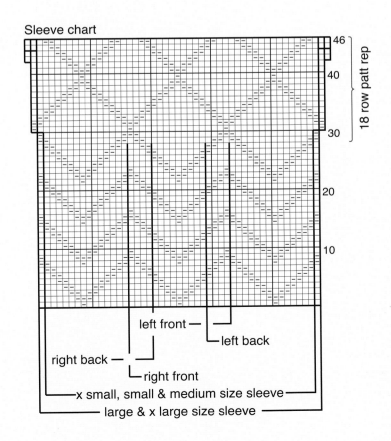

Sleeve chart

18 row patt rep

left front
left back
right back
right front
x small, small & medium size sleeve
large & x large size sleeve

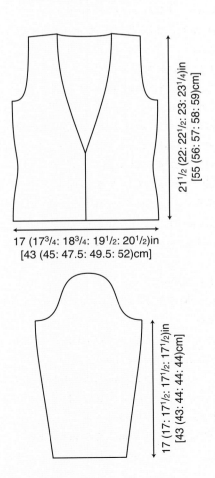

21¹/₂ (22: 22¹/₂: 23: 23¹/₄)in [55 (56: 57: 58: 59)cm]

17 (17³/₄: 18³/₄: 19¹/₂: 20¹/₂)in [43 (45: 47.5: 49.5: 52)cm]

17 (17: 17¹/₂: 17¹/₂: 17¹/₂)in [43 (43: 44: 44: 44)cm]

The unusual vertical stripes and daring color combination give this design an artistic style. The striped jacket and floral pattern on the dress coordinate with each other, bringing to mind avant-garde French artists who looked to the Far East for their inspiration.

YARN AND SIZES

	XS	S	M	L	XL	
To fit bust	32	34	36	38	40	in
	81	86	91	97	102	cm

Rowan Yorkshire Tweed 4 ply

A = light gray (no. 270) or desired 1st CC

5	5	5	5	5	x 25g

B = red (no. 275) or desired 2nd CC

3	3	3	4	4	x 25g

C = medium purple (no. 276) or desired 3rd CC

4	4	4	4	4	x 25g

D = crimson (no. 274) or desired 4th CC

3	4	4	4	4	x 25g

NEEDLES

1 pair size 2 (2³/₄mm) needles
1 pair size 3 (3¹/₄mm) needles

GAUGE/TENSION

25 sts and 38 rows to 4in/10cm measured over pattern using size 3 (3¹/₄mm) needles.

BACK

Cast on 110 (116: 122: 128: 134) sts using size 2 (2³/₄mm) needles and yarn A.
Work in garter st (K every row) for 4 rows, end with a WS row.
Change to size 3 (3¹/₄mm) needles.
Starting and ending rows as indicated, using the **intarsia** technique, working chart rows 1 and 2 **once only** and then repeating chart rows 3 to 10 throughout, cont in patt from chart for body as foll:
Dec 1 st at each end of 17th and every foll 10th row until 100 (106: 112: 118: 124) sts rem.
Work 33 rows, ending with a WS row.

Inc 1 st at each end of next and every foll 10th row until there are 110 (116: 122: 128: 134) sts, taking inc sts into patt.
Work even/straight until back measures 15¹/₂ (15³/₄: 15³/₄: 16: 16)in/39 (40: 40: 41: 41)cm, ending with a WS row.

Shape armholes

Keeping patt correct, bind/cast off 4 (5: 5: 6: 6) sts at beg of next 2 rows, then 3 sts at beg of foll 2 rows.
96 (100: 106: 110: 116) sts.
Dec 1 st at each end of next 3 (3: 5: 5: 7) rows, then on foll 1 (2: 2: 3: 3) alt rows, then on every foll 4th row until 84 (86: 88: 90: 92) sts rem.
Work even/straight until armhole measures 7 (7: 7¹/₂: 7¹/₂: 8)in/18 (18: 19: 19: 20)cm, ending with a WS row.

Shape shoulders and back neck

Bind/cast off 8 (8: 9: 9: 9) sts at beg of next 2 rows.
68 (70: 70: 72: 74) sts.
Next row (RS): Bind/cast off 8 (8: 9: 9: 9) sts, patt until there are 13 (13: 12: 12: 13) sts on right needle and turn, leaving rem sts on a holder.
Work each side of neck separately.
Bind/cast off 4 sts at beg of next row.
Bind/cast off rem 9 (9: 8: 8: 9) sts.
With RS facing, rejoin yarns to rem sts, bind/cast off center 26 (28: 28: 30: 30) sts, patt to end.
Complete to match first side, reversing shapings.

LEFT FRONT

Cast on 58 (61: 64: 67: 70) sts using size 2 (2³/₄mm) needles and yarn A.
Work in garter st for 4 rows, ending with a WS row.

Change to size 3 (3¹/₄mm) needles.
Starting and ending rows as indicated, cont in patt from chart for body as foll:
Row 1 (RS): Work first 55 (58: 61: 64: 67) sts as row 1 of chart, using yarn A K3.
Row 2: Using yarn A K3, work last 55 (58: 61: 64: 67) sts as row 2 of chart.
These 2 rows set the sts—front opening edge 3 sts in garter st using yarn A and all other sts in patt from chart.
Keeping sts correct as now set throughout, dec 1 st at beg of 15th and every foll 10th row until 53 (56: 59: 62: 65) sts rem.
Work 33 rows, ending with a WS row.
Inc 1 st at beg of next and every foll 10th row until there are 58 (61: 64: 67: 70) sts, taking inc sts into patt.
Work even/straight until left front matches back to beg of armhole shaping, ending with a WS row.

Shape armhole

Keeping patt correct, bind/cast off 4 (5: 5: 6: 6) sts at beg of next row, then 3 sts at beg of foll alt row.
51 (53: 56: 58: 61) sts.
Work 1 row.
Dec 1 st at armhole edge of next 3 (3: 5: 5: 7) rows, then on foll 1 (2: 2: 3: 3) alt rows, then on every foll 4th row until 45 (46: 47: 48: 49) sts rem.
Work even/straight until 15 (15: 15: 17: 17) rows less have been worked than on back to start of shoulder shaping, ending with a RS row.

Shape neck

Next row (WS): Patt 11 (12: 12: 12: 12) sts and slip these sts onto a holder, patt to end.

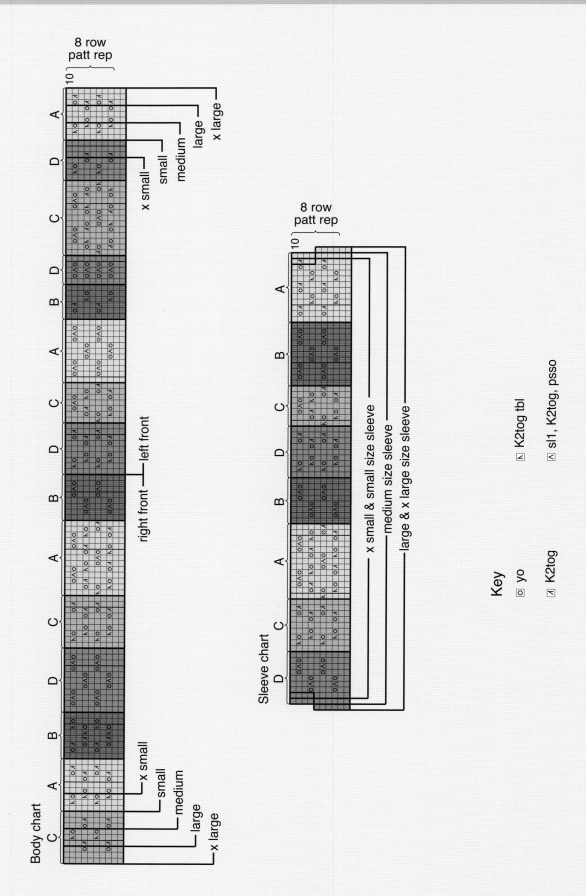

Body chart

Sleeve chart

8 row patt rep

right front — left front

x small
small
medium
large
x large

x small & small size sleeve
medium size sleeve
large & x large size sleeve

Key

⊙ yo

↘ K2tog

↘ K2tog tbl

↗ sl1, K2tog, psso

34 (34: 35: 36: 37) sts.

Keeping patt correct, work 1 row.

Bind/cast off 4 sts at beg of next row.

30 (30: 31: 32: 33) sts.

Dec 1 st at neck edge of next 3 rows, then on foll 2 (2: 2: 3: 3) alt rows. 25 (25: 26: 26: 27) sts.

Work 5 rows, ending with a WS row.

Shape shoulder

Bind/cast off 8 (8: 9: 9: 9) sts at beg of next and foll alt row.

Work 1 row.

Bind/cast off rem 9 (9: 8: 8: 9) sts.

RIGHT FRONT

Cast on 58 (61: 64: 67: 70) sts using size 2 (2³/4mm) needles and yarn A.

Work in garter st for 4 rows, ending with a WS row.

Change to size 3 (3¹/4mm) needles.

Starting and ending rows as indicated, cont in patt from chart for body as foll:

Row 1 (RS): Using yarn A, K3; work last 55 (58: 61: 64: 67) sts as row 1 of chart.

Row 2: Work first 55 (58: 61: 64: 67) sts as row 2 of chart; using yarn A, K3.

These 2 rows set the sts—front opening edge 3 sts in garter st using yarn A and all other sts in patt from chart.

Keeping sts correct as now set throughout, complete to match left front, reversing shapings.

SLEEVES (both alike)

Cast on 76 (76: 78: 80: 80) sts using size 2 (2³/4mm) needles and yarn A.

Work in garter st for 4 rows, ending with a WS row.

Change to size 3 (3¹/4mm) needles.

Starting and ending rows as indicated, using the **intarsia** technique, working chart rows 1 and 2 **once only** and then repeating chart rows 3 to 10 throughout, cont in patt from chart for sleeve as foll:

Dec 1 st at each end of 7th and every foll 10th

row until 66 (66: 68: 70: 70) sts rem.

Work 49 rows, ending with a WS row.

Inc 1 st at each end of next and every foll 10th (8th: 8th: 8th: 6th) row to 72 (72: 80: 82: 84) sts, then on every foll 12th (10th: 10th: 10th: 8th) row until there are 78 (80: 84: 86: 90) sts, taking inc sts into patt.

Work even/straight until sleeve measures 18 (18: 18¹/2: 18¹/2: 18¹/2)in/46 (46: 47: 47: 47)cm, ending with a WS row.

Shape sleeve cap

Keeping patt correct, bind/cast off 4 (5: 5: 6: 6) sts at beg of next 2 rows, then 3 sts at beg of foll 2 rows. 64 (64: 68: 68: 72) sts.

Dec 1 st at each end of next 3 rows, then on foll 4 alt rows, then on every foll 4th row until 40 (40: 44: 44: 48) sts rem.

Work 1 row, ending with a WS row.

Dec 1 st at each end of next and every foll alt row to 30 sts, then on foll 2 rows, ending with a RS row. 26 sts.

Bind/cast off 3 sts at beg of next 4 rows.

Bind/cast off rem 14 sts.

FINISHING

PRESS as described on page 136.

Join both shoulder seams using backstitch, or mattress stitch if preferred.

Neckband

With RS facing, using size 2 (2³/4mm) needles and yarn A, slip 11 (12: 12: 12: 12) sts from right front holder onto right needle, rejoin yarn and pick up and knit 18 (18: 18: 20: 20) sts up right side of neck, 34 (36: 36: 38: 38) sts from back, and 18 (18: 18: 20: 20) sts down left side of neck, then knit across 11 (12: 12: 12: 12) sts left on left front holder.

92 (96: 96: 102: 102) sts.

Work in garter st for 2 rows.

Bind/cast off knitwise (on WS).

See page 136 for finishing instructions, setting in sleeves using the set-in method.

22¹/2 (22³/4: 23¹/4: 23¹/2: 24)in [57 (58: 59: 60: 61)cm]

17¹/2 (18¹/4: 19¹/4: 20: 21)in [44 (46.5: 49: 51: 53.5)cm]

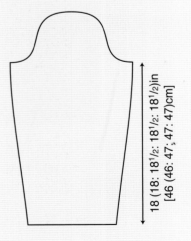

18 (18: 18¹/2: 18¹/2: 18¹/2)in [46 (46: 47: 47: 47)cm]

CHANTEL
KIM HARGREAVES

This crocheted shawl is a true labor of love: once made, it will be treasured forever. The repeated gem-like motif plays with shape and color. Worn here with a slim, pink dress, it's more than an accessory: it lights up the room.

● ●

YARN

Rowan Kid Silk Haze

A = ecru (no. 590) or desired color   1 x 25g

B = gray-lilac (no. 589) or desired color   2 x 25g

C = dark gray (no. 605) or desired color   1 x 25g

D = blue (no. 592) or desired color   1 x 25g

E = light green (no. 581) or desired color   1 x 25g

F = green-blue (no. 582) or desired color   1 x 25g

G = brown (no. 588) or desired color   1 x 25g

H = fuchsia (no. 583) or desired color   1 x 25g

J = grape (no. 600) or desired color   1 x 25g

CROCHET HOOK

Size D-3 (3.00mm) crochet hook

GAUGE/TENSION

One motif measures 3¼in/8.5cm square using
size D-3 (3.00mm) hook.

FINISHED SIZE

Completed shawl measures 17in/43cm wide
and 67in/170cm long, excluding fringe.

CROCHET ABBREVIATIONS

ch = chain

sc = single crochet (double crochet in UK)

dc = double crochet (treble crochet in UK)

tr = treble (double treble in UK)

sp(s) = space(s)

yo = yarn over hook

dc2tog = *yo, insert hook in next dc, yo and
draw a loop through, yo and draw through
2 loops, *skip next 2dc, rep from * to * once
more, yo and draw through all 3 loops on
hook

BASIC MOTIF

Using size D-3 (3.00mm) hook and first color,
ch10 and join with a slip st in first ch to form
a ring.

Round 1 (RS): Ch3 (to count as first dc), 31dc
in ring, join with a slip st in 3rd of 3ch.

Round 2: (Ch7, skip next 3dc, 1 slip st in next
dc) 7 times, ch3, skip next 3dc, 1tr in next dc.
Break off first color and join in 2nd color.

Round 3: Ch3 (to count as first dc), 6dc in tr at
end of previous round, skip 3ch, *7dc in next
ch, skip (3ch, 1 slip st, and 3ch), rep from * to
end, join with a slip st in 3rd of 3ch at beg of
round.

Round 4: 1 slip st in next dc, ch6 (to count as
1dc and 3ch), *skip 1dc, work (1tr, ch5, 1tr) all
in next dc, ch3, skip 1dc, dc2tog over next 4dc,
ch3, skip 1dc, 1sc in next dc, ch3, skip 1dc,**
dc2tog over next 4dc, ch3, rep from * to end,
ending last rep at **, 1dc in next dc, join with a
slip st in 3rd of 6ch at beg of round.
Break off 2nd color and join in 3rd color.

Round 5: Ch1 (does NOT count as st), 1sc in
same place slip st was worked at end of
previous round, *3sc in next ch sp, 1sc in next
tr, 6sc in next ch sp, 1sc in next tr, 3sc in next
ch sp, 1sc in next dc2tog, 3sc in next ch sp, 1sc
in next sc, 3sc in next ch sp,** 1sc in next
dc2tog, rep from * to end, ending last rep at **,
join with a slip st in first sc.

Fasten off.

Basic motif is a square, with 23sc along
each side.

SHAWL

Using colors of yarn at random, make 100 basic
motifs.

Join motifs to form a rectangle 5 motifs wide
and 20 motifs long as foll: holding motifs WS
together and using yarn B, work a row of sc
along edge of motifs, inserting hook through
corresponding sc of both edges.

When all motifs are joined, work one round of
sc using yarn B all around entire outer edge,
ending with a slip st in first sc.

Fasten off.

Cut 13¾in/35cm lengths of yarn B and knot
groups of 5 of these lengths through each ch sp
along ends of shawl to form fringe.

MAGNOLIA
KIM HARGREAVES

A big roll-neck, fastened by large buttons at one side, is the defining feature of this soft, comforting pullover. The subtle juxtaposition of knitwear and a floaty, floral skirt takes one back to an era where femininity had an effortless grace and less of the contrivance of today.

MAGNOLIA
KIM HARGREAVES

YARN AND SIZES

	XS	S	M	L	XL	
To fit bust	32	34	36	38	40	in
	81	86	91	97	102	cm

Rowan Kid Classic and Kid Silk Haze

A = Classic—light blue (no. 822) or desired color

	6	6	6	7	7	x 50g

B = Haze—blue (no. 592) or desired color

	4	4	4	5	5	x 25g

NEEDLES

1 pair size 8 (5mm) needles
1 pair size 9 (5¹/2mm) needles
1 pair size 10 (6mm) needles

BUTTONS—2 buttons (Rowan 00359)

GAUGE/TENSION

16 sts and 20 rows to 4in/10cm measured over St st pattern using size 10 (6mm) needles and ONE STRAND EACH of yarn A and yarn B held tog.

BACK

Cast on 76 (80: 84: 88: 92) sts using size 9 (5¹/2mm) needles and ONE STRAND EACH of yarn A and yarn B.

Row 1 (RS): K1, *P2, K2, rep from * to last 3 sts, P2, K1.

Row 2: P1, *K2, P2, rep from * to last 3 sts, K2, P1.

These 2 rows form rib.

Work in rib for 8 rows more, ending with a WS row.

Change to size 10 (6mm) needles.

Beg with a K row, cont in St st as foll:

Work 2 rows.

Next row (dec) (RS): K2, K2tog, K to last 4 sts, K2tog tbl, K2.

Working all decreases as set by last row, dec 1 st at each end of every foll 6th row until 68 (72: 76: 80: 84) sts rem.

Work 13 rows, ending with a WS row.

Next row (inc) (RS): K2, M1, K to last 2 sts, M1, K2.

Working all increases as set by last row, inc 1 st at each end of every foll 8th row until there are 76 (80: 84: 88: 92) sts.

Work even/straight until back measures 14¹/2 (15: 15: 15¹/2: 15¹/2)in/37 (38: 38: 39: 39)cm, ending with a WS row.

Shape armholes

Bind/cast off 4 sts at beg of next 2 rows.

68 (72: 76: 80: 84) sts.

Dec 1 st at each end of next 5 (5: 7: 7: 9) rows, then on foll 0 (1: 1: 2: 2) alt rows, then on foll 4th row. 56 (58: 58: 60: 60) sts.

Work even/straight until armhole measures 8¹/2 (8¹/2: 9: 9: 9¹/2)in/22 (22: 23: 23: 24)cm, ending with a WS row.

Shape shoulders and back neck

Bind/cast off 4 sts at beg of next 2 rows.

48 (50: 50: 52: 52) sts.

Next row (RS): Bind/cast off 4 sts, K until there are 7 sts on right needle and turn, leaving rem sts on a holder.

Work each side of neck separately.

Bind/cast off 4 sts at beg of next row.

Bind/cast off rem 3 sts.

With RS facing, rejoin yarns to rem sts, bind/cast off center 26 (28: 28: 30: 30) sts, K to end.

Complete to match first side, reversing shapings.

FRONT

Work as given for back until 10 (10: 10: 12: 12) rows less have been worked than on back to start of shoulder shaping, ending with a WS row.

Shape neck

Next row (RS): K17 (17: 17: 18: 18) and turn, leaving rem sts on a holder.

Work each side of neck separately.

Dec 1 st at neck edge of next 4 rows, then on foll 2 (2: 2: 3: 3) alt rows. 11 sts.

Work 1 row, ending with a WS row.

Shape shoulder

Bind/cast off 4 sts at beg of next and foll alt row.

Work 1 row. Bind/cast off rem 3 sts.

With RS facing, rejoin yarns to rem sts, bind/cast off center 22 (24: 24: 24: 24) sts, K to end.

Complete to match first side, reversing shapings.

SLEEVES (both alike)

Cast on 48 (48: 48: 50: 50) sts using size 9 (5¹/2mm) needles and ONE STRAND EACH of yarn A and yarn B.

Row 1 (RS): P1 (1: 1: 2: 2), K2, *P2, K2, rep from * to last 1 (1: 1: 2: 2) sts, P1 (1: 1: 2: 2).

Row 2: K1 (1: 1: 2: 2), P2, *K2, P2, rep from * to last 1 (1: 1: 2: 2) sts, K1 (1: 1: 2: 2).

These 2 rows form rib.

Work in rib for 18 rows more, ending with a WS row.

Change to size 10 (6mm) needles.

Beg with a K row, cont in St st as foll:

Work 4 rows.

Next row (inc) (RS): K2, M1, K to last 2 sts, M1, K2.

Working all increases as set by last row, inc 1 st at each end of every foll 20th (20th: 16th: 20th: 16th) row to 54 (54: 54: 58: 56) sts, then on every foll 18th (18th: 14th: -: 14th) row until there are 56 (56: 58: -: 60) sts.

Work even/straight until sleeve measures 18 (18: 18¹/2: 18¹/2: 18¹/2)in/46 (46: 47: 47: 47)cm, ending with a WS row.

Shape sleeve cap

Bind/cast off 4 sts at beg of next 2 rows.

48 (48: 50: 50: 52) sts.

Dec 1 st at each end of next 3 rows, then on foll alt row, then on every foll 4th row until 32 (32: 34: 34: 36) sts rem.

Work 1 row, ending with a WS row.

Dec 1 st at each end of next and every foll alt row to 28 sts, then on foll 5 rows, ending with a WS row.

Bind/cast off rem 18 sts.

FINISHING

PRESS as described on page 136.

Join both shoulder seams using backstitch, or mattress stitch if preferred.

Collar

Cast on 90 (98: 98: 106: 106) sts using size 8 (5mm) needles and ONE STRAND EACH of yarn A and yarn B.

Row 1 (RS): K2, (P1, K1) 3 times, P2, *K2, P2, rep from * to last 8 sts, (K1, P1) 3 times, K2.

Row 2: (K1, P1) 4 times, K2, *P2, K2, rep from * to last 8 sts, (P1, K1) 4 times.

These 2 rows form rib.

Work in rib for 10 rows more.

Change to size 10 (6mm) needles.

Work 4 rows, ending with a WS row.

Row 17 (RS): Rib 18, M1, rib 2, M1, rib 30 (34: 34: 38: 38), M1, rib 2, M1, rib to end. 94 (102: 102: 110: 110) sts.

Keeping rib correct, work 3 rows.

Row 21: Rib 19, M1, rib 2, M1, rib 32 (36: 36: 40: 40), M1, rib 2, M1, rib to end. 98 (106: 106: 114: 114) sts.

Keeping rib correct, work 3 rows.

Row 25: Rib 20, M1, rib 2, M1, rib 34 (38: 38: 42: 42), M1, rib 2, M1, rib to end. 102 (110: 110: 118: 118) sts.

Keeping rib correct, work 3 rows.

Row 29: Rib 21, M1, rib 2, M1, rib 36 (40: 40: 44: 44), M1, rib 2, M1, rib to end. 106 (114: 114: 122: 122) sts.

Keeping rib correct, work 3 rows.

Bind/cast off loosely in rib.

See page 136 for finishing instructions, setting in sleeves using the set-in method.

Overlap ends of collar for 8 sts and sew cast-on edge of collar to neck edge, positioning shaped sections at shoulder seams. Using photograph as a guide, attach buttons through both layers of collar.

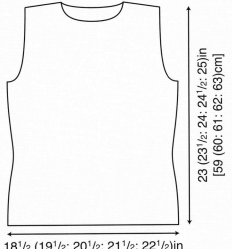

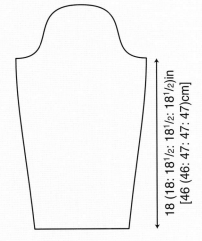

23 (23^1/$_2$: 24: 24^1/$_2$: 25)in [59 (60: 61: 62: 63)cm]

18 (18: 18^1/$_2$: 18^1/$_2$: 18^1/$_2$)in [46 (46: 47: 47: 47)cm]

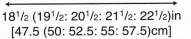

18^1/$_2$ (19^1/$_2$: 20^1/$_2$: 21^1/$_2$: 22^1/$_2$)in [47.5 (50: 52.5: 55: 57.5)cm]

JOY
KIM HARGREAVES

Inspired by French films, this cardigan combines refinement and naivety with
its petite collar and neat buttons. The pleated skirt carries through the slim line.
The ankle socks and classic beret complete the girlish look.

YARN AND SIZES

	XS	S	M	L	XL	
To fit bust	32	34	36	38	40	in
	81	86	91	97	102	cm

Rowan Yorkshire Tweed 4 ply

	10	10	11	11	12	x 25g

Use gray-lilac (no. 268) or desired color

NEEDLES

1 pair size 1 (2³/₄mm) needles
1 pair size 2 (3mm) needles
1 pair size 3 (3¹/₄mm) needles

EXTRAS—8 buttons (Rowan 00322); and approx 5,300 beads (Rowan 01020)

GAUGE/TENSION

26 sts and 38 rows to 4in/10cm measured over patterned St st using size 3 (3¹/₄mm) needles.

SPECIAL ABBREVIATIONS

Bead 1 = place a bead by bringing yarn to front (RS) of work and slipping bead up next to st just worked, slip next st purlwise from left needle to right needle and take yarn back to back (WS) of work, leaving bead sitting in front of slipped st on RS. Do not place beads on edge sts of rows as this will obstruct seams.

Beading note: Before starting to knit, thread beads onto yarn. To do this, thread a fine sewing needle with sewing thread. Knot ends of thread and then pass end of yarn through this loop. Thread a bead onto sewing thread and then gently slide it along and onto knitting yarn. Continue in this way until required number of beads are on yarn.

BACK

Cast on 113 (119: 127: 133: 141) sts using size 2 (3mm) needles.
Row 1 (RS): K0 (1: 1: 0: 0), *P1, K1, rep from * to last 1 (0: 0: 1: 1) st, P1 (0: 0: 1: 1).

Rows 2 and 3: P0 (1: 1: 0: 0), *K1, P1, rep from * to last 1 (0: 0: 1: 1) st, K1 (0: 0: 1: 1).
Row 4: As row 1.
These 4 rows form seed/moss st.
Work in seed/moss st for a 2 rows more, ending with a WS row.
Change to size 3 (3¹/₄mm) needles.
Cont in seed/moss st for 14 rows more, ending with a WS row.
Counting in from both ends of last row, place markers on 28th (29th: 31st: 32nd: 34th) st in from ends of row.
Next row (dec) (RS): Work 2 tog, *patt to within 1 st of marked st, work 3 tog (marked st is center st of these 3 sts), rep from * once more, patt to last 2 sts, work 2 tog.
107 (113: 121: 127: 135) sts.
Work 9 rows.
Rep last 10 rows 3 times more, ending with a WS row.
89 (95: 103: 109: 117) sts.
Purl 2 rows.
Starting and ending rows as indicated and repeating the 12 patt rows throughout, cont in patt from chart for body as foll:
Inc 1 st at each end of 3rd and every foll 4th row to 101 (107: 115: 121: 129) sts, then on every foll 6th row until there are 113 (119: 127: 133: 141) sts.
Work even/straight until back measures 13¹/₂ (14: 14¹/₄: 14³/₄: 14³/₄)in/35 (36: 36: 37: 37)cm, ending with a WS row.

Shape armholes

Keeping patt correct, bind/cast off 4 (5: 5: 6: 6) sts at beg of next 2 rows.
105 (109: 117: 121: 129) sts.
Dec 1 st at each end of next 5 (5: 7: 7: 9) rows, then on foll 5 (6: 6: 7: 7) alt rows. 85 (87: 91: 93: 97) sts.
Work even/straight until armhole measures 8 (8: 8¹/₄: 8¹/₄: 8¹/₂)in/20 (20: 21: 21: 22)cm, ending with a WS row.

Shape shoulders and back neck

Bind/cast off 8 (8: 9: 9: 9) sts at beg of next 2 rows. 69 (71: 73: 75: 79) sts.

Next row (RS): Bind/cast off 8 (8: 9: 9: 9) sts, patt until there are 12 (12: 12: 12: 14) sts on right needle and turn, leaving rem sts on a holder.
Work each side of neck separately.
Bind/cast off 4 sts at beg of next row.
Bind/cast off rem 8 (8: 8: 8: 10) sts.
With RS facing, rejoin yarn to rem sts, bind/cast off center 29 (31: 31: 33: 33) sts, patt to end.
Complete to match first side, reversing shapings.

LEFT FRONT

Cast on 60 (63: 67: 70: 74) sts using size 2 (3mm) needles.
Row 1 (RS): K0 (1: 1: 0: 0), *P1, K1, rep from * to end.
Row 2: *P1, K1, rep from * to last 0 (1: 1: 0: 0) st, P0 (1: 1: 0: 0).
Row 3: P0 (1: 1: 0: 0), *K1, P1, rep from * to end.
Row 4: *K1, P1, rep from * to last 0 (1: 1: 0: 0) st, K0 (1: 1: 0: 0).
These 4 rows form seed/moss st.
Work in seed/moss st for 2 rows more, ending with a WS row.
Change to size 3 (3¹/₄mm) needles.
Cont in seed/moss st for 14 rows more, ending with a WS row.
Counting in from end of last row, place marker on 28th (29th: 31st: 32nd: 34th) st in from end of row.
Next row (dec) (RS): Work 2 tog, patt to within 1 st of marked st, work 3 tog (marked st is center st of these 3 sts), patt to end. 57 (60: 64: 67: 71) sts.
Work 9 rows.
Rep last 10 rows 3 times more, ending with a WS row. 48 (51: 55: 58: 62) sts.
Purl 2 rows.
Starting and ending rows as indicated and repeating the 12 patt rows throughout, cont in patt from chart for body as foll:
Row 1 (RS): Work first 42 (45: 49: 52: 56) sts as row 1 of chart, seed/moss st 6 sts.
Row 2: Seed/moss st 6 sts, work last 42 (45: 49: 52: 56) sts as row 2 of chart.
These 2 rows set the sts—front opening edge 6

sts still in seed/moss st with rem sts in patt from chart.

Cont as set, inc 1 st at beg of next and every foll 4th row to 54 (57: 61: 64: 68) sts, then on every foll 6th row until there are 60 (63: 67: 70: 74) sts. Work even/straight until left front matches back to beg of armhole shaping, ending with WS row.

Shape armhole

Keeping patt correct, bind/cast off 4 (5: 5: 6: 6) sts at beg of next row. 56 (58: 62: 64: 68) sts. Work 1 row.

Dec 1 st at armhole edge of next 5 (5: 7: 7: 9) rows, then on foll 5 (6: 6: 7: 7) alt rows. 46 (47: 49: 50: 52) sts.

Work even/straight until 34 (36: 36: 38: 38) rows less have been worked than on back to start of shoulder shaping, ending with WS row.

Shape for collar

Next row (RS): Patt to last 7 sts, seed/moss st 7 sts.
Next row: Seed/moss st 7 sts, patt to end.
Next row: Patt to last 8 sts, seed/moss st 8 sts.
Next row: Seed/moss st 8 sts, patt to end.
Next row: Patt to last 9 sts, seed/moss st 9 sts.
Next row: Seed/moss st 9 sts, patt to end.

Cont in this way, working one st more in seed/moss st at front opening edge on next and every foll alt row until the foll row has been worked:

Next row (WS): Seed/moss st 22 (23: 23: 24: 24) sts, patt to end.

Keeping sts correct as now set, work 2 rows more, ending with a WS row.

Shape shoulder

Bind/cast off 8 (8: 9: 9: 9) sts at beg of next and foll alt row, then 8 (8: 8: 8: 10) sts at beg of foll alt row. 22 (23: 23: 24: 24) sts. Work 1 row, ending with a WS row.

Break yarn and leave sts on a holder.

Mark positions for 8 buttons along left front opening edge—first to come in row 45, last to come 1in/2.5cm below start of collar shaping, and rem 6 buttons evenly spaced between.

RIGHT FRONT

Cast on 60 (63: 67: 70: 74) sts using size 2 (3mm) needles.

Row 1 (RS): *K1, P1, rep from * to last 0 (1: 1: 0: 0) st, K0 (1: 1: 0: 0).
Row 2: P0 (1: 1: 0: 0), *K1, P1, rep from * to end.
Row 3: *P1, K1, rep from * to last 0 (1: 1: 0: 0) st, P0 (1: 1: 0: 0).
Row 4: K0 (1: 1: 0: 0), *P1, K1, rep from * to end.

These 4 rows form seed/moss st.

Work in seed/moss st for 2 rows more, ending with a WS row.

Change to size 3 (3¼mm) needles.

Cont in seed/moss st for 14 rows more, ending with a WS row.

Counting in from beg of last row, place marker on 28th (29th: 31st: 32nd: 34th) st in from beg of row.

Next row (dec) (RS): Patt to within 1 st of marked st, work 3 tog (marked st is center st of these 3 sts), patt to last 2 sts, work 2 tog.

57 (60: 64: 67: 71) sts.

Work 9 rows.

Rep last 10 rows twice more, and then first of these rows (the dec row) again.

48 (51: 55: 58: 62) sts.

Work 3 rows.

Next row (buttonhole row) (RS): Patt 2 sts, work 2 tog, yo (to make a buttonhole), patt to end.

Work 5 rows more, ending with a WS row.

Purl 2 rows.

Starting and ending rows as indicated and repeating the 12 patt rows throughout, cont in patt from chart for body as foll:

Row 1 (RS): Seed/moss st 6 sts, work last 42 (45: 49: 52: 56) sts as row 1 of chart.
Row 2: Work first 42 (45: 49: 52: 56) sts as row 2 of chart, seed/moss st 6 sts.

These 2 rows set the sts—front opening edge 6 sts still in seed/moss st with rem sts in patt from chart.

Complete to match left front, reversing shapings and with the addition of 7 buttonholes more worked to correspond with positions marked on left front for buttons. When right front is complete, ending with a WS row, do NOT break off yarn. Set this ball of yarn to one side for collar.

SLEEVES (both alike)

Cast on 61 (61: 63: 65: 65) sts using size 3 (3¼mm) needles.

Beg with a K row, work in St st for 2 rows, ending with a WS row.

Starting and ending rows as indicated and

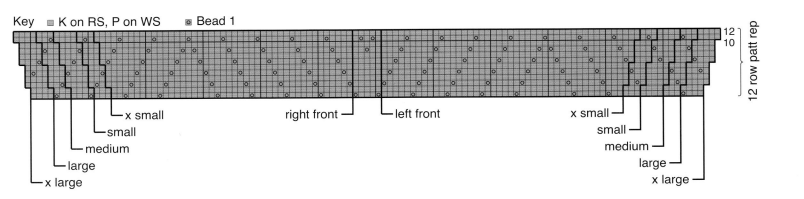

Key ▩ K on RS, P on WS   ◉ Bead 1

x small · small · medium · large · x large · right front · left front · x small · small · medium · large · x large

12 · 10 · 12 row patt rep

repeating the 12 patt rows throughout, cont in patt from chart for sleeve as foll:

Inc 1 st at each end of 29th and every foll 12th (12th: 10th: 10th: 10th) row to 77 (67: 87: 89: 73) sts, then on every foll 10th (10th: 8th: 8th: 8th) row until there are 83 (85: 89: 91: 95) sts, taking inc sts into patt.

Work even/straight until sleeve measures 17 (17: 17½: 17½: 17½)in/43 (43: 44: 44: 44)cm, ending with a WS row.

Shape sleeve cap

Keeping patt correct, bind/cast off 4 (5: 5: 6: 6) sts at beg of next 2 rows.

75 (75: 79: 79: 83) sts.

Dec 1 st at each end of next 5 rows, then on foll 3 alt rows, then on every foll 4th row until 45 (45: 49: 49: 53) sts rem.

Work 1 row, ending with a WS row.

Dec 1 st at each end of next and every foll alt row to 35 sts, then on foll 3 rows, ending with a WS row. Bind/cast off rem 29 sts.

CUFFS (both alike)

Cast on 65 (65: 67: 69: 69) sts using size 1 (2¾mm) needles.

Row 1 (RS): P1, *K1, P1, rep from * to end.

Rows 2 and 3: K1, *P1, K1, rep from * to end.

Row 4: As row 1.

These 4 rows form seed/moss st.

Work in seed/moss st for 2 rows more, ending with a WS row.

Starting and ending rows as indicated, cont in patt from chart for cuff as foll:

Row 1 (RS): Seed/moss st 5 sts, work next 55 (55: 57: 59: 59) sts as row 1 of chart, seed/moss st rem 5 sts.

Row 2: Seed/moss st 5 sts, work next 55 (55: 57: 59: 59) sts as row 2 of chart, seed/moss st rem 5 sts. These 2 rows set the sts—5 sts still in seed/moss st at each end and rem sts in patt foll chart. Cont as set until all 24 rows of chart have been completed, ending with a WS row. Bind/cast off.

FINISHING

PRESS as described on page 136.

Join both shoulder seams using backstitch, or mattress stitch if preferred.

Collar

With RS facing, using size 2 (3mm) needles and ball of yarn left with right front, patt across 22 (23: 23: 24: 24) sts on right front holder, pick up and knit 37 (39: 39: 41: 41) sts from back, then patt across 22 (23: 23: 24: 24) sts on left front holder. 81 (85: 85: 89: 89) sts.

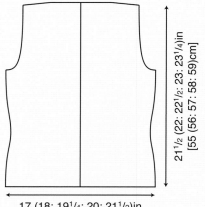

17 (18: 19¼: 20: 21½)in
[43.5 (46: 49: 51: 54)cm]

21½ (22: 22½: 23: 23¼)in
[55 (56: 57: 58: 59)cm]

Work in seed/moss st as set by front sts for 1¼in/3cm, ending with a WS row.

Bind/cast off in seed/moss st.

See page 136 for finishing instructions, setting in sleeves using the set-in method. Overlap ends of cuffs for 2 sts and sew together at bound-off/cast-off edge. With RS of cuff against WS of sleeve and ends of cuffs 2¾in/7cm back from sleeve seam, sew bound-off/cast-off edge of cuffs to cast-on edge of sleeves.

Fold cuff to RS.

17 (17: 17½: 17½: 17½)in
[43 (43: 44: 44: 44)cm]

Sleeve chart

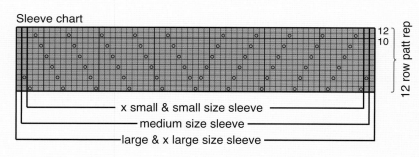

12
10

12 row patt rep

x small & small size sleeve
medium size sleeve
large & x large size sleeve

Cuff chart

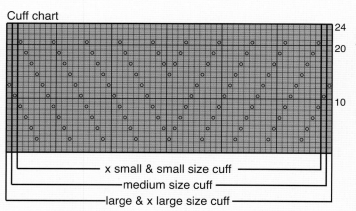

24
20

10

x small & small size cuff
medium size cuff
large & x large size cuff

PIERS
MARTIN STOREY

Wrap-over necks were a hallmark of the '50s and '60s. This hunky sweater, with its repeated motifs of fir trees and snowflakes, takes its inspiration from alpine winters, spent in wooden chalets fringed with icicles. It's a real open-air look that brings to mind the crunch of snow underfoot and the stars in the night sky.

PIERS
MARTIN STOREY

YARN AND SIZES

	S	M	L	XL	XXL	
To fit chest	38	40	42	44	46	in
	97	102	107	112	117	cm

Rowan Yorkshire Tweed DK

A = off-white (no. 352) or desired MC

	10	11	11	12	12	x 50g

B = medium brown (no. 355) or desired 1st CC

	3	3	3	3	3	x 50g

C = light brown (no. 353) or desired 2nd CC

	2	2	2	2	2	x 50g

NEEDLES

1 pair size 3 (3¼mm) needles
1 pair size 6 (4mm) needles
Size 3 (3¼mm) circular needle

GAUGE/TENSION

22 sts and 29 rows to 4in/10cm measured over patterned St st using 4mm (size 6) needles.

BACK

Cast on 111 (117: 123: 129: 135) sts using size 3 (3¼mm) needles and yarn A.
Row 1 (RS): P3, *K3, P3, rep from * to end.
Row 2: K3, *P3, K3, rep from * to end.
These 2 rows form rib. Cont in rib for 23 rows more, ending with a RS row.
Row 26 (WS): Rib 6 (4: 7: 6: 4), M1, *rib 11 (12: 12: 13: 14), M1, rep from * to last 6 (5: 8: 6: 5) sts, rib to end. 121 (127: 133: 139: 145) sts.
Change to size 6 (4mm) needles.
Starting and ending rows as indicated, using the **intarsia** technique and repeating the 76 row patt repeat throughout, cont in patt from chart, which is worked entirely in St st beg with a K row, as foll:
Work even/straight until back measures 17 (17: 17½: 17½: 17¾)in/43 (43: 44: 44: 45)cm, ending with a WS row.

Shape armholes

Keeping patt correct, bind/cast off 6 (6: 7: 7: 8) sts at beg of next 2 rows.

109 (115: 119: 125: 129) sts.**
Dec 1 st at each end of next 3 (5: 5: 7: 7) rows, then on foll 3 (3: 4: 4: 5) alt rows, then on foll 4th row. 95 (97: 99: 101: 103) sts.
Work even/straight until armhole measures 8½ (9: 9: 9½: 9½)in/22 (23: 23: 24: 24)cm, ending with a WS row.

Shape shoulders and back neck

Bind/cast off 10 sts at beg of next 2 rows.
75 (77: 79: 81: 83) sts.
Next row (RS): Bind/cast off 10 sts, patt until there are 14 (14: 15: 15: 15) sts on right needle and turn, leaving rem sts on a holder.
Work each side of neck separately.
Bind/cast off 4 sts at beg of next row.
Bind/cast off rem 10 (10: 11: 11: 11) sts.
With RS facing, rejoin yarns to rem sts, bind/cast off center 27 (29: 29: 31: 33) sts, patt to end.
Complete to match first side, reversing shapings.

FRONT

Work as given for back to **, ending with a WS row.
Dec 1 st at each end of next 3 (5: 5: 7: 7) rows, then on foll 3 (3: 4: 4: 4) alt rows, then on foll 4th (4th: 0: 0: 0) row. 95 (97: 101: 103: 107) sts.
Work 3 (1: 3: 1: 1) rows, end with a WS row.

Divide for neck

Next row (RS): (K2tog) 0 (0: 1: 0: 1) times, patt 31 (32: 32: 35: 35) sts and turn, leaving rem sts on a holder. 31 (32: 33: 35: 36) sts.
Work each side of neck separately.
Dec 1 st at armhole edge on 0 (0: 0: 2nd: 4th) row **and at same time** dec 1 st at neck edge on 22nd (16th: 16th: 12th: 10th) and every foll 0 (16th: 16th: 12th: 10th) row until 30 (30: 31: 31: 31) sts rem.
Work even/straight until front matches back to start of shoulder shaping, end with a WS row.

Shape shoulder

Bind/cast off 10 sts at beg of next and foll alt row.
Work 1 row. Bind/cast off rem 10 (10: 11: 11: 11) sts.

With RS facing, rejoin yarns to rem sts, bind/cast off center 33 sts, patt to last 0 (0: 2: 0: 2) sts, (K2tog) 0 (0: 1: 0: 1) times.
Complete to match first side, reversing shapings.

SLEEVES (both alike)

Cast on 51 (51: 53: 55: 55) sts using size 3 (3¼mm) needles and yarn A.
Row 1 (RS): P0 (0: 1: 2: 2), K3, *P3, K3, rep from * to last 0 (0: 1: 2: 2) sts, P0 (0: 1: 2: 2).
Row 2: K0 (0: 1: 2: 2), P3, *K3, P3, rep from * to last 0 (0: 1: 2: 2) sts, K0 (0: 1: 2: 2).
These 2 rows form rib.
Cont in rib for 23 rows more, ending with a RS row.
Row 26 (WS): Rib 3 (3: 4: 5: 5), M1, *rib 9, M1, rep from * to last 3 (3: 4: 5: 5) sts, rib to end.
57 (57: 59: 61: 61) sts.
Change to size 6 (4mm) needles.
Starting and ending rows as indicated, cont in patt from chart, shaping sides by inc 1 st at each end of 7th (7th: 7th: 7th: 5th) and every foll 6th (6th: 6th: 6th: 4th) row to 87 (91: 93: 93: 65) sts, then on every foll 8th (-: -: 8th: 6th) row until there are 89 (-: -: 95: 97) sts, taking inc sts into patt.
Work even/straight until sleeve measures 19 (19¼: 19¼: 19½: 19½)in/48 (49: 49: 50: 50)cm, ending with a WS row.

Shape sleeve cap

Keeping patt correct, bind/cast off 6 (6: 7: 7: 8) sts at beg of next 2 rows.
77 (79: 79: 81: 81) sts.
Dec 1 st at each end of next 5 rows, then on foll 3 alt rows, then on every foll 4th row until 53 (55: 55: 57: 57) sts rem.
Work 1 row, ending with a WS row.
Dec 1 st at each end of next and every foll alt row to 47 sts, then on foll 7 rows, ending with a WS row. 33 sts.
Bind/cast off 5 sts at beg of next 2 rows.
Bind/cast off rem 23 sts.

FINISHING

PRESS as described on page 136.

Join both shoulder seams using backstitch.

Collar

With RS facing, using size 3 (3¹/₄mm) circular needle and yarn A, pick up and knit 45 (47: 47: 49: 49) sts up right side of neck, 39 (41: 41: 43: 43) sts from back, then 45 (47: 47: 49: 49) sts down left side of neck.

129 (135: 135: 141: 141) sts.

Beg with row 2, work in rib as given for back for 6in/15cm.

Bind/cast off in rib.

Overlap ends of collar and sew to front neck bound-off/cast-off sts.

See page 136 for finishing instructions, setting in sleeves using the set-in method.

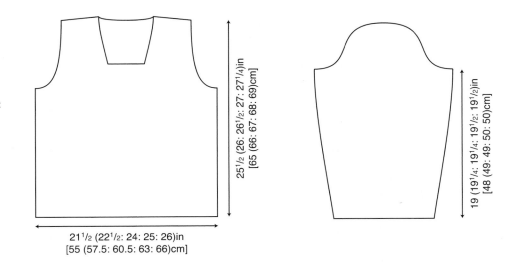

25¹/₂ (26: 26¹/₂: 27: 27¹/₄)in
[65 (66: 67: 68: 69)cm]

21¹/₂ (22¹/₂: 24: 25: 26)in
[55 (57.5: 60.5: 63: 66)cm]

19 (19¹/₄: 19¹/₄: 19¹/₂: 19¹/₂)in
[48 (49: 49: 50: 50)cm]

Key ☐ A ▣ B ▦ C

76 row pattern repeat

small
medium
large
x large
xx large

small & medium size sleeve
large size sleeve
x large & xx large size sleeve

small
medium
large
x large
xx large

MONETTE
LUCINDA GUY

This small, floaty scarf is fine and feminine.
Delightfully fluffy, it is light enough to be worn with a dress or blouse.
The lace edge enhances the delicate look of something precious.

YARN

Rowan Kid Silk Haze

A = orange (no. 596) or desired MC   2 x 25g

B = cherry (no. 606) or desired CC   1 x 25g

NEEDLES

1 pair size 3 (3¹/₄mm) needles

GAUGE/TENSION

25 sts and 34 rows to 4in/10cm measured over
St st using size 3 (3¹/₄mm) needles.

FINISHED SIZE

Completed scarf measures 8in/20cm wide and
59in/150cm long.

SCARF

First section

Cast on 51 sts using size 3 (3¹/₄mm) needles
and yarn A.

Row 1 (RS): K1, *yo, K3, sl 1, K2tog, psso,
K3, yo, K1, rep from * to end.

Row 2: Purl.

Row 3: As row 1.

Row 4: Knit.

Rows 5 to 8: As rows 1 to 4.

Rows 9 to 14: Knit.

Join in yarn B.

Rows 15 and 16: Using yarn B, knit.

Rows 17 and 18: Using yarn A, knit.

Rows 19 to 22: As rows 15 to 18.

Rows 23 and 24: As rows 15 and 16.

Row 25: Using yarn A, knit.

Row 26: Using yarn A, purl.

Rows 27 to 38: As rows 15 to 26.

Rows 39 and 40: As rows 15 and 16.

Row 41: Using yarn A, knit.

Row 42: Using yarn A, purl.

Row 43: Using yarn B, knit.

Row 44: Using yarn B, purl.

Rep rows 41 to 44 **only** until first section
measures 29¹/₂in/75cm, ending after row 43.**
Break yarn and leave sts on a holder.

Second section

Work as given for first section to **.

Join sections

Holding sections RS together and using yarn B,
bind/cast off sts of both sections together.

FINISHING

PRESS as described on page 136.

CHERIE

KIM HARGREAVES

The boyish look of this sweater, with its decorative buttons, creates the impression that it's been borrowed from a brother or boyfriend, or raided from clothes stashed away in the attic. It's a look that, paradoxically, enhances the femininity of the wearer—especially when, as here, it's worn next to the skin.

YARN AND SIZES

	XS	S	M	L	XL	
To fit bust	32	34	36	38	40	in
	81	86	91	97	102	cm

Rowan Yorkshire Tweed DK

	9	9	10	10	11	x 50g

Use dark gray-blue (no. 354) or desired color

NEEDLES

1 pair size 5 (3¾mm) needles

1 pair size 6 (4mm) needles

BUTTONS—3 buttons (Rowan 00347)

GAUGE/TENSION

20 sts and 28 rows to 4in/10cm measured over St st using size 6 (4mm) needles.

BACK and FRONT (both alike)

Cast on 91 (95: 101: 105: 111) sts using size 5 (3¾mm) needles.

Row 1 (RS): K1, *P1, K1, rep from * to end.

Row 2: P1, *K1, P1, rep from * to end.

These 2 rows form rib.

Work in rib for 24 rows more, dec 1 st at each end of 19th row and ending with a WS row.

89 (93: 99: 103: 109) sts.

Change to size 6 (4mm) needles.

Beg with a K row, cont in St st as foll:

Work 4 rows.

Next row (dec) (RS): K2, K2tog, K to last 4 sts, K2tog tbl, K2.

Working all decreases as set by last row, dec 1 st at each end of foll 10th row.

85 (89: 95: 99: 105) sts.

Work 19 rows, ending with a WS row.

Next row (inc) (RS): K2, M1, K to last 2 sts, M1, K2.

Working all increases as set by last row, inc 1 st at each end of every foll 8th row until there are 95 (99: 105: 109: 115) sts.

Work even/straight until work measures 13¾in/35cm, ending with a WS row.

CHERIE
KIM HARGREAVES

Shape raglan armholes

Bind/cast off 5 sts at beg of next 2 rows.

85 (89: 95: 99: 105) sts.

XL size only

Next row (RS): K2, K2tog, K to last 4 sts,
K2tog tbl, K2.

Next row: P2, P2tog tbl, P to last 4 sts,
P2tog, P2. 101 sts.

All sizes

Working all raglan decreases in same way
as side seam decreases, dec 1 st at each end
of next and 3 (3: 1: 1: 0) foll 4th rows, then
on every foll alt row until 37 (39: 39:
41: 41) sts rem.

Work 1 row, ending with a WS row.

Bind/cast off.

SLEEVES (both alike)

Cast on 69 (69: 71: 73: 73) sts using size 5
(3³/₄mm) needles.

Work in rib as given for back for 32 rows, dec
1 st at each end of 17th and foll 10th row and
ending with a WS row.

65 (65: 67: 69: 69) sts.

Change to size 6 (4mm) needles.

Beg with a K row and working all sleeve
seam decreases and increases and raglan
decreases in same way as for back and front,
cont in St st as foll:

Dec 1 st at each end of 5th and every foll 8th
row until 59 (59: 61: 63: 63) sts rem.

Work 15 rows, ending with a WS row.

Inc 1 st at each end of next and every foll
16th (12th: 14th: 14th: 12th) row to 67 (69:
67: 69: 69) sts, then on every foll - (-: 12th:
12th: 10th) row until there are - (-: 71:
73: 75) sts.

Work even/straight until sleeve measures 18
(18: 18¹/₂: 18¹/₂: 18¹/₂)in/46 (46: 47: 47: 47)cm,
ending with a WS row.

Shape raglan

Bind/cast off 5 sts at beg of next 2 rows.

57 (59: 61: 63: 65) sts.

Dec 1 st at each end of next and every foll 4th
row to 41 (43: 45: 47: 49) sts, then on every
foll alt row until 17 sts rem.

Work 1 row, ending with a WS row.

Bind/cast off.

FINISHING

PRESS as described on page 136.

Join both back and right front raglan
seams using backstitch, or mattress stitch
if preferred.

Neckband

With RS facing and using size 5 (3³/₄mm)
needles, pick up and knit 36 (38: 38: 40: 40) sts
from front, 15 sts from right sleeve (place
marker on center st of these 15 sts), 37 (39: 39:
41: 41) sts from back, and 15 sts from left
sleeve (place marker on center st of these
15 sts), then turn and cast on 6 sts.

109 (113: 113: 117: 117) sts.

Row 1 (WS): K1, *P1, K1, rep from * to end.

Row 2: K2, *P1, K1, rep from * to last st, K1.

These 2 rows form rib.

Work in rib for 1 row more.

Row 4 (RS): *Rib to within 4 sts of marked st,
work 2 tog tbl, rib 5 (marked st is center st of
these 5 sts), work 2 tog, rep from * once more,
rib to end.

Work 3 rows.

Rep last 4 rows once more.

101 (105: 105: 109: 109) sts.

Row 12 (RS): *Rib to within 5 sts of marked
st, work 3 tog tbl, rib 5 (marked st is center st
of these 5 sts), work 3 tog, rep from * once
more, rib to end.

93 (97: 97: 101: 101) sts.

Work 5 rows.

Bind/cast off in rib.

See page 136 for finishing instructions.

Overlap ends of neckband for 6 sts and sew
cast-on edge of neckband to inside of neck
edge. Using photograph as a guide, attach
buttons through both layers of neckband.

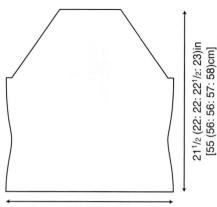

21¹/₂ (22: 22: 22¹/₂: 23)in
[55 (56: 56: 57: 58)cm]

18¹/₂ (19¹/₂: 20¹/₂: 21¹/₂: 22¹/₂)in
[47.5 (49.5: 52.5: 54.5: 57.5)cm]

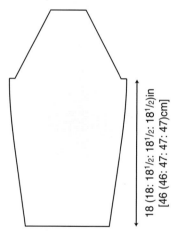

18 (18: 18¹/₂: 18¹/₂: 18¹/₂)in
[46 (46: 47: 47: 47)cm]

ORIEL

KIM HARGREAVES

This neat little jacket, with its asymmetrical fastening, has a flattering neckline
edged with a crocheted trim. The slightly boxy shape of the garment makes it perfect
for teaming with a wide '50s style printed skirt. Here, a blouse with a lacy collar
adds a finishing touch.

YARN AND SIZES

	XS	S	M	L	XL	
To fit bust	32	34	36	38	40	in
	81	86	91	97	102	cm

Rowan Yorkshire Tweed 4 ply
and Kid Silk Haze

A = 4 ply—light gray (no. 270) or desired color

9	10	10	11	11	x 25g

B = Haze—dark gray (no. 605) or desired color

5	5	5	6	6	x 25g

C = 4 ply—charcoal (no. 277) or desired color

1	1	1	1	1	x 25g

D = Haze—grape (no. 600) or desired color

1	1	1	1	1	x 25g

NEEDLES AND CROCHET HOOK

1 pair size 5 (3³/₄mm) needles
1 pair size 6 (4mm) needles
Size C-2 (2.50mm) crochet hook

BUTTONS—2 buttons (Rowan 00348)

GAUGE/TENSION

23 sts and 30 rows to 4in/10cm measured over
St st using size 6 (4mm) needles and ONE
STRAND EACH of yarn A and yarn B held tog.

CROCHET ABBREVIATIONS

sc = single crochet (double crochet in UK)
ch = chain.

BACK

Cast on 105 (111: 117: 123: 129) sts using
size 5 (3³/₄mm) needles and ONE STRAND
EACH of yarn A and yarn B.
Beg with a K row, work in St st for 6 rows,
ending with a WS row.
Change to size 6 (4mm) needles.
Cont in St st until back measures 10¹/₂ (11: 11:
11¹/₄: 11¹/₂)in/27 (28: 28: 29: 29)cm, ending
with a WS row.

Shape armholes

Bind/cast off 3 (4: 4: 5: 5) sts at beg of next 2
rows. 99 (103: 109: 113: 119) sts.
Dec 1 st at each end of next 5 (5: 7: 7: 9) rows,
then on foll 5 (6: 6: 7: 7) alt rows.
79 (81: 83: 85: 87) sts.
Work even/straight until armhole measures 8 (8:
8¹/₄: 8¹/₄: 8¹/₂)in/20 (20: 21: 21: 22)cm, ending
with a WS row.

Shape shoulders and back neck

Bind/cast off 7 (7: 7: 7: 8) sts at beg of next 2
rows.
65 (67: 69: 71: 71) sts.
Next row (RS): Bind/cast off 7 (7: 7: 7: 8) sts, K
until there are 11 (11: 12: 12: 11) sts on right
needle and turn, leaving rem sts on a holder.
Work each side of neck separately.
Bind/cast off 4 sts at beg of next row.
Bind/cast off rem 7 (7: 8: 8: 7) sts.
With RS facing, rejoin yarns to rem sts, bind/cast
off center 29 (31: 31: 33: 33) sts,
K to end.
Complete to match first side, reversing shapings.

LEFT FRONT

Cast on 70 (73: 76: 79: 82) sts using size 5
(3³/₄mm) needles and ONE STRAND EACH of
yarn A and yarn B.
Beg with a K row, work in St st for 6 rows,
ending with a WS row.
Change to size 6 (4mm) needles.
Cont in St st until left front matches back to beg
of armhole shaping, ending with a WS row.

Shape armhole

Bind/cast off 3 (4: 4: 5: 5) sts at beg of next row.
67 (69: 72: 74: 77) sts.
Work 1 row.
Dec 1 st at armhole edge of next 5 (5: 7: 7: 9)
rows, then on foll 5 (6: 6: 7: 7) alt rows.
57 (58: 59: 60: 61) sts.
Work even/straight until 29 (29: 29: 31: 31) rows
less have been worked than on back to start of
shoulder shaping, ending with a RS row.

Shape neck

Bind/cast off 7 (8: 8: 8: 8) sts at beg of next row,
6 sts at beg of foll alt row, then 4 sts at beg of
foll 3 alt rows. 32 (32: 33: 34: 35) sts.
Dec 1 st at neck edge on next 6 rows, then on
foll 5 (5: 5: 6: 6) alt rows.
21 (21: 22: 22: 23) sts.
Work 4 rows, ending with a WS row.

Shape shoulder

Bind/cast off 7 (7: 7: 7: 8) sts at beg of next
and foll alt row. Work 1 row.
Bind/cast off rem 7 (7: 8: 8: 7) sts.

RIGHT FRONT

Work to match left front, reversing shapings
and with the addition of one buttonhole worked
6 rows before start of neck shaping as foll:
Buttonhole row (RS): K3, bind/cast off 2 sts
(to make a buttonhole—cast on 2 sts over these
bound-off/cast-off sts in next row), K to end,
working armhole dec if appropriate.

SLEEVES (both alike)

Cast on 55 (55: 57: 59: 59) sts using size 5
(3³/₄mm) needles and ONE STRAND EACH
of yarn A and yarn B.
Beg with a K row, work in St st for 6 rows,
ending with a WS row.
Change to size 6 (4mm) needles.
Cont in St st for 18 rows more, ending with a
WS row.
Next row (RS): K2, M1, K to last 2 sts,
M1, K2.
Working all increases as set by last row, cont
in St st, shaping sides by inc 1 st at each end
of every foll 10th (10th: 10th: 10th: 8th) row
to 63 (75: 73: 75: 67) sts, then on every foll
12th (-: 12th: 12th: 10th) row until there are
73 (-: 77: 79: 81) sts.
Work even/straight until sleeve measures 17
(17: 17¹/₂: 17¹/₂: 17¹/₂)in/43 (43: 44: 44: 44)cm,
ending with a WS row.

Shape sleeve cap

Bind/cast off 3 (4: 4: 5: 5) sts at beg of next 2
rows. 67 (67: 69: 69: 71) sts.

Dec 1 st at each end of next 3 rows, then on foll 2 alt rows, then on every foll 4th row until 45 (45: 47: 47: 49) sts rem.

Work 1 row, ending with a WS row.

Dec 1 st at each end of next and every foll alt row to 41 sts, then on foll 5 rows, ending with a WS row. Bind/cast off rem 31 sts.

FINISHING

PRESS as described on page 136.

See page 136 for finishing instructions, setting in sleeves using the set-in method.

Edging

With RS facing, using size C-2 (2.50mm) crochet hook and yarn ONE STRAND of yarn C, attach yarn at base of one side seam and work one round of sc even/straightly around entire hem, front opening, and neck edges, working 3sc in corners to ensure edging lays flat and ending with a slip st in first sc.

Round 2 (RS): Ch1 (does NOT count as st), 1sc in each sc to end, working extra sc and skipping sc as required to ensure that edging lays flat, join with a slip st in first sc.

Rep last round once more, ensuring that there is a multiple of 6 sts at end of round.

Break off yarn C and join in ONE STRAND of yarn D.

Round 4 (RS): *1 slip st in each of next 3sc, insert hook into round 3 directly below st just worked and draw a loop through, insert hook into round 2 one st further along and draw a loop through, insert hook into round 3 one st further along and draw a loop through, yo and draw through all 4 loops on hook, skip 1sc, 1 slip st in each of next 2sc, rep from * to end, join with a slip st in first slip st. Fasten off.

Work edging around lower edge of sleeves in same way.

Attach button to RS of left front to correspond with buttonhole. Make button loop at top of left front opening edge and attach button to inside of right front to correspond.

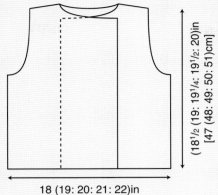

18 (19: 20: 21: 22)in
[45.5 (48.5: 51: 53.5: 56)cm]

(18½ (19: 19¼: 19½: 20)in
[47 (48: 49: 50: 51)cm]

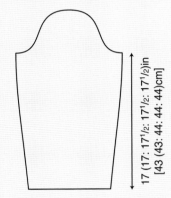

17 (17: 17½: 17½: 17½)in
[43 (43: 44: 44: 44)cm]

SALINA
KIM HARGREAVES

If anything epitomizes the knitwear of the '50s it's the button-opening and collar used for this classic pullover. Matched here with a daringly printed full skirt, it has a feel best summed up as *ingenue*, a French word that describes childlike innocence.

SALINA
KIM HARGREAVES

YARN AND SIZES

	XS	S	M	L	XL	
To fit bust	32	34	36	38	40	in
	81	86	91	97	102	cm

Rowan Felted Tweed

	6	6	6	7	7	x 50g

Use green (no. 146) or desired color

NEEDLES

1 pair size 3 (3^1/$_4$mm) needles
1 pair size 5 (3^3/$_4$mm) needles

BUTTONS—4 buttons (Rowan 00320)

GAUGE/TENSION

23 sts and 32 rows to 4in/10cm measured over
St st using size 5 (3^3/$_4$mm) needles.

BACK

Cast on 93 (99: 105: 111: 117) sts using
size 3 (3^1/$_4$mm) needles.
Row 1 (RS): K1, *P1, K1, rep from * to end.
Row 2: As row 1.
These 2 rows form seed/moss st. Cont in
seed/moss st for 14 rows more, ending with a
WS row.
Change to size 5 (3^3/$_4$mm) needles.
Beg with a K row, cont in St st as foll:
Work 4 rows.
Next row (RS): K2, K2tog, K to last 4 sts,
K2tog tbl, K2.
Working all decreases as set by last row, dec 1
st at each end of every foll 6th row until 81 (87:
93: 99: 105) sts rem.
Work 15 rows, ending with a WS row.
Next row (RS): K2, M1, K to last 2 sts, M1,
K2.
Working all increases as set by last row, inc 1 st
at each end of every foll 6th row until there are
97 (103: 109: 115: 121) sts.
Work even/straight until back measures 13^1/$_2$
(14: 14^1/$_4$: 14^3/$_4$: 14^3/$_4$)in/35 (36: 36: 37: 37)cm,
ending with a WS row.

Shape armholes

Bind/cast off 4 (5: 5: 6: 6) sts at beg of next 2
rows. 89 (93: 99: 103: 109) sts.
Dec 1 st at each end of next 3 (3: 5: 5: 7) rows,
then on foll 2 (3: 3: 4: 4) alt rows, then on every
foll 4th row until 75 (77: 79: 81: 83) sts rem.
Work even/straight until armhole measures 8
(8: 8^1/$_4$: 8^1/$_4$: 8^1/$_2$)in/20 (20: 21: 21: 22)cm,
ending with a WS row.

Shape shoulders and back neck

Bind/cast off 7 (7: 7: 7: 8) sts at beg of next 2
rows. 61 (63: 65: 67: 67) sts.
Next row (RS): Bind/cast off 7 (7: 7: 7: 8) sts,
K until there are 11 (11: 12: 12: 11) sts on right
needle and turn, leaving rem sts on a holder.
Work each side of neck separately.
Bind/cast off 4 sts at beg of next row.
Bind/cast off rem 7 (7: 8: 8: 7) sts.
With RS facing, rejoin yarn to rem sts,
bind/cast off center 25 (27: 27: 29: 29) sts,
K to end.
Complete to match first side, reversing
shapings.

FRONT

Work as given for back to beg of armhole
shaping, ending with a WS row.

Shape armholes and divide for front opening

Next row (RS): Bind/cast off 4 (5: 5: 6: 6) sts,
K until there are 42 (44: 47: 49: 52) sts on right
needle and turn, leaving rem sts on a holder.
Work each side of front separately.
Next row (WS): Cast on 5 sts and work across
these 5 sts as foll: P1, (K1, P1) twice, P to end.
47 (49: 52: 54: 57) sts.
Keeping front opening edge 5 sts in seed/moss
st as now set, cont as foll:
Dec 1 st at armhole edge of next 3 (3: 5: 5: 7)
rows, then on foll 2 (3: 3: 4: 4) alt rows, then
on every foll 4th row until 40 (41: 42: 43: 44)
sts rem.
Work 22 (20: 18: 16: 14) rows, ending with a
RS row.

Shape lapel

Next row (WS): Seed/moss st 6 sts, P to end.
Next row: K to last 7 sts, seed/moss st 7 sts.
Next row: Seed/moss st 8 sts, P to end.
Next row: K to last 9 sts, seed/moss st 9 sts.
Next row: Seed/moss st 10 sts, P to end.
Cont in this way, working one extra st in
seed/moss st on every row until there are 18
(19: 19: 20: 20) sts in seed/moss st.
Now keeping sts correct as set, work
even/straight until 7 rows less have been
worked than on back to start of shoulder
shaping, ending with a RS row.
Next row (WS): Seed/moss st 19 (20: 20: 21:
21) sts, P to end.
Keeping sts correct as now set, work 6 rows
more, ending with a WS row.

Shape shoulder

Bind/cast off 7 (7: 7: 7: 8) sts at beg of next
and foll alt row, then 7 (7: 8: 8: 7) sts at beg of
foll alt row.
19 (20: 20: 21: 21) sts.
Work 1 row, ending with a WS row.
Break yarn and leave sts on a holder.
With RS facing, rejoin yarn to rem sts, (P1,
K1) twice, P1, K to end.
Keeping front opening edge 5 sts in seed/moss
st as now set, cont as foll:
Bind/cast off 4 (5: 5: 6: 6) sts at beg of next
row. 47 (49: 52: 54: 57) sts.
Dec 1 st at armhole edge of next 3 (3: 5: 5: 6)
rows, then on foll 1 (1: 0: 0: 0) alt rows.
43 (45: 47: 49: 51) sts.
Work 1 (1: 1: 1: 0) row, ending with a WS row.
Next row (buttonhole row) (RS): P1, K1, yo,
K2tog (to make a buttonhole), P1, K to last 2
sts, K2tog.
42 (44: 46: 48: 50) sts.
Dec 1 st at armhole edge on 4th (2nd: 2nd:
2nd: 2nd) and foll 0 (0: 1: 2: 3) alt rows, then
on 1 (2: 2: 2: 2) foll 4th rows and at same time
make 1 (1: 1: 1: 2) buttonholes more as before
in 8th and foll 0 (0: 0: 0: 8th) row.

40 (41: 42: 43: 44) sts.

Work 22 (20: 18: 16: 14) rows, making 2 (2: 2: 2: 1) buttonholes more in 8th (6th: 4th: 2nd: 8th) and foll 8th (8th: 8th: 8th: 0) row and ending with a RS row. (4 buttonholes made.)

Shape lapel

Next row (WS): P to last 6 sts, seed/moss st 6 sts.

Next row: Seed/moss st 7 sts, K to end.

Next row: P to last 8 sts, seed/moss st 8 sts.

Next row: Seed/moss st 9 sts, K to end.

Next row: P to last 10 sts, seed/moss st 10 sts.

Cont in this way, working one extra st in seed/moss st on every row until there are 18 (19: 19: 20: 20) sts in seed/moss st.

Now keeping sts correct as set, work even/straight until 7 rows less have been worked than on back to start of shoulder shaping, ending with a RS row.

Next row (WS): P to last 19 (20: 20: 21: 21) sts, seed/moss st to end.

Keeping sts correct as now set, work 7 rows more, ending with a RS row.

Shape shoulder

Bind/cast off 7 (7: 7: 7: 8) sts at beg of next and foll alt row, then 7 (7: 8: 8: 7) sts at beg of foll alt row.

19 (20: 20: 21: 21) sts.

Do NOT break yarn but leave sts on a holder—this ball of yarn will be used for collar.

SLEEVES (both alike)

Cast on 57 (57: 59: 61: 61) sts using size 5 (3³/₄mm) needles.

Beg with a K row, work in St st for 12 (10: 10: 10: 10) rows, ending with a WS row.

Next row (RS): K2, M1, K to last 2 sts, M1, K2.

Working all increases as set by last row, inc 1 st at each end of every foll 12th (10th: 10th: 10th: 10th) row to 69 (65: 65: 67: 79) sts, then on every foll 14th (12th: 12th: 12th: 12th) row until there are 73 (75: 77: 79: 81) sts.

Work even/straight until sleeve measures 14

(14: 14¹/₂: 14¹/₂: 14¹/₂)in/36 (36: 37: 37: 37)cm, ending with a WS row.

Shape sleeve cap

Bind/cast off 4 (5: 5: 6: 6) sts at beg of next 2 rows.

65 (65: 67: 67: 69) sts.

Dec 1 st at each end of next 3 rows, then on foll 2 alt rows, then on every foll 4th row until 43 (43: 45: 45: 47) sts rem.

Work 1 row, ending with a WS row.

Dec 1 st at each end of next and every foll alt row to 37 sts, then on foll 5 rows, end with a WS row. Bind/cast off rem 27 sts.

FINISHING

PRESS as described on page 136.

Join both shoulder seams using backstitch.

Collar

With RS facing, using size 3 (3¹/₄mm) needles and ball of yarn left with right front, seed/moss

st 19 (20: 20: 21: 21) sts of right front, pick up and knit 33 (35: 35: 37: 37) sts from back, then seed/moss st 19 (20: 20: 21: 21) sts of left front.

71 (75: 75: 79: 79) sts.

Cont in seed/moss st as set for 1¹/₄in/3cm.

Bind/cast off in seed/moss st.

Cuffs (both alike)

Cast on 63 (63: 65: 67: 67) sts using size 3 (3¹/₄mm) needles.

Work in seed/moss st as given for back for 3in/7.5cm.

Bind/cast off in seed/moss st.

See page 136 for finishing instructions, setting in sleeves using the set-in method. Sew cast-on edge of left front opening border in place on inside. Overlap ends of cuffs for 3 sts, then sew cast-on edge of cuff to lower edge of sleeve, positioning overlap directly opposite sleeve seam. Fold cuff to RS.

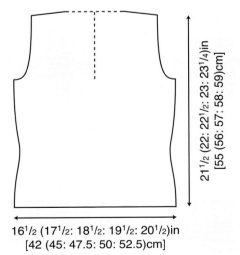

16¹/₂ (17¹/₂: 18¹/₂: 19¹/₂: 20¹/₂)in
[42 (45: 47.5: 50: 52.5)cm]

21¹/₂ (22: 22¹/₂: 23: 23³/₄)in
[55 (56: 57: 58: 59)cm]

14 (14: 14¹/₂: 14¹/₂: 14¹/₂)in
[36 (36: 37: 37: 37)cm]

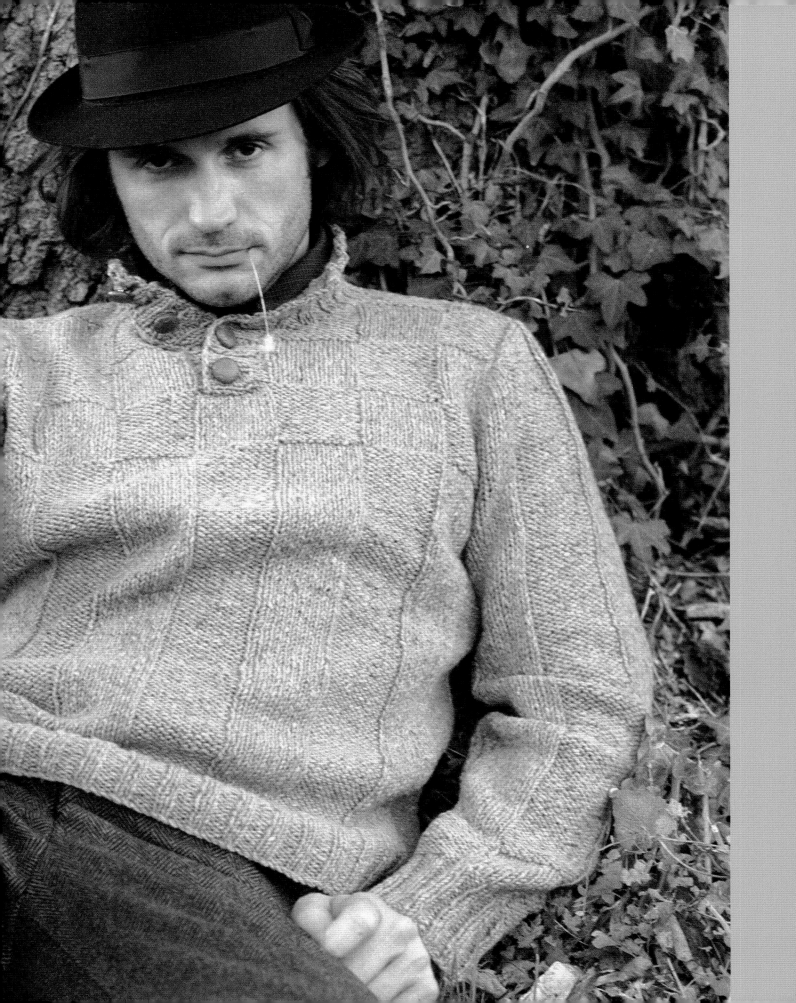

BEAU

KIM HARGREAVES

A rustic woven effect and tweed yarn give this
sweater a rugged appearance echoing the texture of
tree bark and woodland floor. Once again, the button
neckline is used to effect for a classic of bygone times.
The chunky buttons complete the look.

YARN AND SIZES

	S	M	L	XL	XXL	
To fit chest	38	40	42	44	46	in
	97	102	107	112	117	cm

Rowan Yorkshire Tweed Aran

	7	7	7	8	8	x 100g

Use camel (no. 413) or desired color

NEEDLES

1 pair size 6 (4mm) needles
1 pair size 8 (5mm) needles

BUTTONS—4 buttons (Rowan 00341)

GAUGE/TENSION

16 sts and 23 rows to 4in/10cm measured over
St st using size 8 (5mm) needles.

BACK

Cast on 90 (94: 98: 102: 106) sts using size 6
(4mm) needles.
Row 1 (RS): K0 (2: 0: 2: 0), P2, *K2, P2, rep
from * to last 0 (2: 0: 2: 0) sts, K0 (2: 0: 2: 0).
Row 2: P0 (2: 0: 2: 0), K2, *P2, K2, rep from *
to last 0 (2: 0: 2: 0) sts, P0 (2: 0: 2: 0).
Rep rows 1 and 2 nine times more, ending with
a WS row.
Change to size 8 (5mm) needles.
Starting and ending rows as indicated, rep chart
rows 1 and 2 for body until back measures 16^3/$_4$
(17: 17^1/$_2$: 17^1/$_2$: 17^3/$_4$)in/43 (43: 44: 44: 45)cm,
ending with a WS row.
Now repeating chart rows 3 to 30 throughout,
cont as foll:
Shape armholes
Keeping patt correct, bind/cast off 5 sts at beg
of next 2 rows. 80 (84: 88: 92: 96) sts.
Dec 1 st at each end of next 5 (5: 7: 7: 9) rows,
then on foll 2 (3: 2: 3: 2) alt rows.
66 (68: 70: 72: 74) sts.
Work even/straight until armhole measures 8^3/$_4$
(9: 9: 9^1/$_2$: 9^1/$_2$)in/22 (23: 23: 24: 24)cm, ending
with a WS row.

BEAU
KIM HARGREAVES

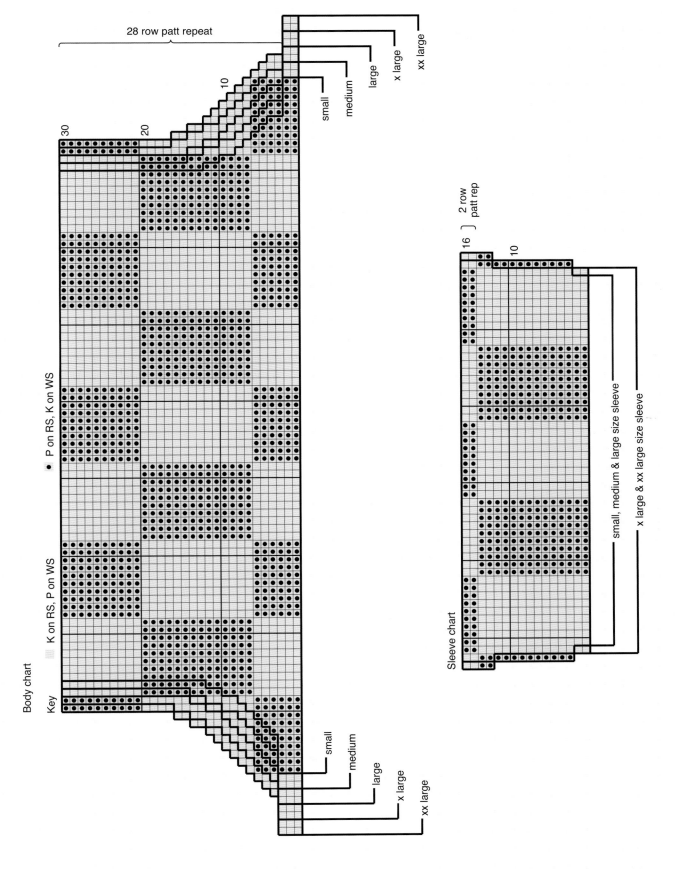

28 row patt repeat

30

20

10

small
medium
large
x large
xx large

small
medium
large
x large
xx large

Body chart

Key

K on RS, P on WS

● P on RS, K on WS

2 row patt rep

16

10

Sleeve chart

small, medium & large size sleeve

x large & xx large size sleeve

BEAU
KIM HARGREAVES

Shape shoulders and back neck

Bind/cast off 6 (6: 7: 7: 7) sts at beg of next 2 rows.

54 (56: 56: 58: 60) sts.

Next row (RS): Bind/cast off 6 (6: 7: 7: 7) sts, patt until there are 11 (11: 10: 10: 10) sts on right needle and turn, leaving rem sts on a holder.

Work each side of neck separately.

Bind/cast off 4 sts at beg of next row.

Bind/cast off rem 7 (7: 6: 6: 6) sts.

With RS facing, rejoin yarn to rem sts, bind/cast off center 20 (22: 22: 24: 26) sts, patt to end.

Complete to match first side, reversing shapings.

FRONT

Work as given for back until 34 (34: 36: 36: 36) rows less have been worked than on back to start of shoulder shaping, ending with a WS row.

Divide for front opening

Next row (RS): Patt 30 (31: 32: 33: 34) sts and turn, leaving rem sts on a holder.

Work each side of neck separately.

Work 18 rows, ending with a RS row.

Shape neck

Keeping patt correct, bind/cast off 3 (4: 3: 4: 5) sts at beg of next row. 27 (27: 29: 29: 29) sts.

Dec 1 st at neck edge of next 6 rows, then on foll 2 (2: 3: 3: 3) alt rows. 19 (19: 20: 20: 20) sts.

Work 4 rows, ending with a WS row.

Shape shoulder

Bind/cast off 6 (6: 7: 7: 7) sts at beg of next and foll alt row.

Work 1 row. Bind/cast off rem 7 (7: 6: 6: 6) sts.

With RS facing, rejoin yarn to rem sts, bind/cast off center 6 sts, patt to end.

Complete to match first side, reversing shapings.

SLEEVES (both alike)

Cast on 48 (48: 48: 50: 50) sts using size 6 (4mm) needles.

Row 1 (RS): K1 (1: 1: 2: 2), P2, *K2, P2, rep from * to last 1 (1: 1: 2: 2) sts, K1 (1: 1: 2: 2).

Row 2: P1 (1: 1: 2: 2), K2, *P2, K2, rep from * to last 1 (1: 1: 2: 2) sts, P1 (1: 1: 2: 2).

These 2 rows form rib.

Cont in rib for 18 rows more, ending with a WS row.

Change to size 8 (5mm) needles.

Starting and ending rows as indicated and working chart rows 1 and 14 once only and then repeating chart rows 15 and 16 as required, cont in patt from chart for sleeve as foll:

Inc 1 st at each end of 3rd and every foll 10th row to 66 (58: 58: 58: 58) sts, then on every foll - (8th: 8th: 8th: 8th) row until there are - (68: 68: 70: 70) sts, taking inc sts into patt.

Work even/straight until sleeve measures 19¼ (19½: 19½: 20: 20)in/49 (50: 50: 51: 51)cm, ending with a WS row.

Shape sleeve cap

Keeping patt correct, bind/cast off 5 sts at beg of next 2 rows. 56 (58: 58: 60: 60) sts.

Dec 1 st at each end of next 3 rows, then on foll 1 (2: 2: 3: 3) alt rows, then on every foll 4th row until 38 sts rem.

Work 1 row, ending with a WS row.

Dec 1 st at each end of next 6 rows, ending with a WS row. Bind/cast off rem 26 sts.

FINISHING

PRESS as described on page 136.

Join both shoulder seams using backstitch.

Neckband

With RS facing and using size 6 (4mm) needles, pick up and knit 21 (22: 22: 23: 24) sts up right side of neck, 28 (30: 30: 32: 34) sts from back, then 21 (22: 22: 23: 24) sts down left side of neck.

70 (74: 74: 78: 82) sts.

Row 1 (WS): P2, *K2, P2, rep from * to end.

Row 2: K2, *P2, K2, rep from * to end.

Cont in rib until neckband measures 3¼in/8cm.

Bind/cast off in rib.

Button band

With RS facing and using size 6 (4mm) needles, pick up and knit 32 sts up right front opening edge, between bound-off/cast-off sts at base of opening and top of neckband.

Row 1 (WS): *K2, P2, rep from * to end.

This row forms rib.

Work in rib for 8 rows more. Bind/cast off in rib.

Buttonhole band

With RS facing and using size 6 (4mm) needles, pick up and knit 32 sts down left front opening edge, between top of neckband and bound-off/cast-off sts at base of opening.

Row 1 (WS): *P2, K2, rep from * to end.

Work in rib for 3 rows more.

Row 5 (WS): Rib 2, *work 2 tog, yo (to make a buttonhole), rib 6, rep from * twice more, work 2 tog, yo (to make 4th buttonhole), rib 4.

Work in rib for 4 rows more.

Bind/cast off in rib.

Lay buttonhole band over button band and stitch in place to bound-off/cast-off sts at base of opening. See page 136 for finishing instructions, setting in sleeves using the set-in method.

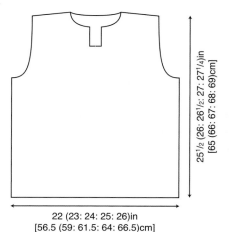

22 (23: 24: 25: 26)in
[56.5 (59: 61.5: 64: 66.5)cm]

25½ (26: 26½: 27: 27¼)in [65 (66: 67: 68: 69)cm]

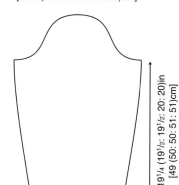

19¼ (19½: 19½: 20: 20)in [49 (50: 50: 51: 51)cm]

AGNES

KIM HARGREAVES

This top, with its figure-hugging shape and banded effect, enhances a curvy hour-glass figure. The opening in the sleeves is a cheeky revealing touch that balances the demure neckline that frames the face.

AGNES
KIM HARGREAVES

YARN AND SIZES

	XS	S	M	L	XL	
To fit bust	32	34	36	38	40	in
	81	86	91	97	102	cm

Rowan 4 ply Soft

| | 6 | 6 | 7 | 7 | 7 | x 50g |

Use medium blue (no. 369) or desired color

NEEDLES

1 pair size 2 (2³/₄mm) needles
1 pair size 3 (3¹/₄mm) needles

RIBBON—48(52: 52: 56: 56)in/120 (130: 130: 140: 140)cm of ¹/₂in/1cm wide fancy ribbon

GAUGE/TENSION

28 sts and 46 rows to 4in/10cm measured over seed/moss stitch, 28 sts and 36 rows to 4in/10cm measured over St st using size 3 (3¹/₄mm) needles.

BACK

Cast on 121 (127: 135: 141: 149) sts using size 2 (2³/₄mm) needles.
Row 1 (RS): K0 (1: 5: 0: 0), (P1, K1) 1 (2: 2: 0: 2) times, P1, *K7, (P1, K1) twice, P1, rep from * to last 10 (1: 5: 8: 0) sts, K7 (1: 5: 7: 0), (P1, K1) 1 (0: 0: 0: 0) times, P1 (0: 0: 1: 0).
Row 2: P0 (1: 5: 0: 0), (P1, K1) 1 (2: 2: 0: 2) times, P1, *P7, (P1, K1) twice, P1, rep from * to last 10 (1: 5: 8: 0) sts, P7 (1: 5: 7: 0), (P1, K1) 1 (0: 0: 0: 0) times, P1 (0: 0: 1: 0).
These 2 rows form patt.
Work in patt for 6 rows more, ending with a WS row.
Change to size 3 (3¹/₄mm) needles. Cont in patt for 8 rows more, ending with a WS row.
Counting in from both ends of last row, place markers on 22nd (25th: 29th: 32nd: 36th) and 34th (37th: 41st: 44th: 48th) sts in from both ends of last row. (4 marked sts.)
Next row (dec) (RS): (Patt to within 2 sts of marked st, K2tog) twice, (patt to marked st,

K marked st, K2tog tbl) twice, patt to end.
Work 7 rows.
Rep last 8 rows 3 times more, and then first of these rows (the dec row) again.
101 (107: 115: 121: 129) sts.
Work 19 rows, ending with a WS row.
Next row (inc) (RS): (Patt to marked st, M1, K marked st) twice, (patt to marked st, K marked st, M1) twice, patt to end.
Work 9 rows.
Rep last 10 rows 3 times more, and then first of these rows (the inc row) again.
121 (127: 135: 141: 149) sts.
Work even/straight until back measures 14 (14¹/₄: 14¹/₄: 14¹/₂: 14³/₄)in/35 (36: 36: 37: 37)cm, ending with a WS row.
Shape armholes
Keeping patt correct, bind/cast off 5 (6: 6: 7: 7) sts at beg of next 2 rows.
111 (115: 123: 127: 135) sts.
Dec 1 st at each end of next 5 (5: 7: 7: 9) rows, then on foll 4 (5: 5: 6: 6) alt rows.
93 (95: 99: 101: 105) sts.
Next row (WS): P1 (0: 0: 1: 1), *K1, P1, rep from * to last 0 (1: 1: 0: 0) st, K0 (1: 1: 0: 0).
Next row: P1 (0: 0: 1: 1), *K1, P1, rep from * to last 0 (1: 1: 0: 0) st, K0 (1: 1: 0: 0).
Last 2 rows form seed/moss st.
Cont in seed/moss st until armhole measures 7 (7: 7¹/₂: 7¹/₂: 7³/₄)in/18 (18: 19: 19: 20)cm, ending with a WS row.
Shape shoulders and back neck
Bind/cast off 7 (7: 8: 8: 9) sts at beg of next 2 rows.
79 (81: 83: 85: 87) sts.
Next row (RS): Bind/cast off 7 (7: 8: 8: 9) sts, seed/moss st until there are 12 sts on right needle and turn, leaving rem sts on a holder.
Work each side of neck separately.
Bind/cast off 4 sts at beg of next row.
Bind/cast off rem 8 sts.
With RS facing, rejoin yarn to rem sts, bind/cast off center 41 (43: 43: 45: 45) sts,

seed/moss st to end.
Complete to match first side.

FRONT

Work as given for back until 28 (28: 28: 30: 30) rows less have been worked than on back to start of shoulder shaping, ending with a WS row.
Shape front neck
Next row (RS): Seed st 36 (36: 38: 39: 41) sts and turn, leaving rem sts on a holder.
Work each side of neck separately.
Dec 1 st at neck edge of next 8 rows, then on foll 5 (5: 5: 6: 6) alt rows, then on foll 4th row.
22 (22: 24: 24: 26) sts.
Work 5 rows, ending with a WS row.
Shape shoulder
Bind/cast off 7 (7: 8: 8: 9) sts at beg of next and foll alt row.
Work 1 row. Bind/cast off rem 8 sts.
With RS facing, rejoin yarn to rem sts, bind/cast off center 21 (23: 23: 23: 23) sts, seed/moss st to end.
Complete to match first side.

SLEEVES (both alike)

Cast on 79 (81: 85: 87: 91) sts using size 2 (2³/₄mm) needles.
Work in garter st (K every row) for 3 rows.
Change to size 3 (3¹/₄mm) needles.
Row 4 (eyelet row) (WS): K1, *yo, K2tog, rep from * to end.
Change to size 2 (2³/₄mm) needles.
Work in garter st for 2 rows.
Change to size 3 (3¹/₄mm) needles.
Row 7 (RS): Knit.
Row 8: P1, *K1, P1, rep from * to end.
Row 8 sets position of seed/moss st.
Keeping seed/moss st correct throughout, cont as foll:
Divide for opening
Next row (RS): Seed/moss st 39 (40: 42: 43: 45) sts and turn, leaving rem sts on a holder.

Work each side of sleeve separately.

Work 1 row, ending with a WS row.

Inc 1 st at beg of next and every foll 6th row until there are 43 (44: 46: 47: 49) sts.

Work 7 rows, ending with a WS row.

Shape sleeve cap

Bind/cast off 5 (6: 6: 7: 7) sts at beg of next row.

38 (38: 40: 40: 42) sts.

Work 1 row.

Dec 1 st at beg of next row and at same edge on foll 2 rows, then on foll 2 alt rows, then on foll 4th row.

32 (32: 34: 34: 36) sts.

Work 1 row, ending with a WS row.

Break yarn and leave sts on a second holder.

With RS facing, rejoin yarn to sts left on first holder, work 2 tog, seed/moss st to end.

39 (40: 42: 43: 45) sts.

Work 1 row, ending with a WS row.

Inc 1 st at end of next and every foll 6th row until there are 43 (44: 46: 47: 49) sts.

Work 8 rows, ending with a WS row.

Shape sleeve cap

Bind/cast off 5 (6: 6: 7: 7) sts at beg of next row. 38 (38: 40: 40: 42) sts.

Dec 1 st at end of next row and at same edge on foll 2 rows, then on foll 2 alt rows, then on foll 4th row. 32 (32: 34: 34: 36) sts.

Work 1 row, ending with a WS row.

Break yarn.

Join sections

Next row (RS): Seed/moss st across first 31 (31: 33: 33: 35) sts of first section, inc in last st, then seed/moss st across 32 (32: 34: 34: 36) sts of second section.

65 (65: 69: 69: 73) sts.

Work 1 row, ending with a WS row.

Dec 1 st at each end of next and foll 4th row, then on every foll 6th row to 57 (57: 61: 61: 65) sts, then on foll 4th row.

55 (55: 59: 59: 63) sts.

Work 3 rows, ending with a WS row.

Dec 1 st at each end of next and every foll alt row to 47 sts, then on foll 5 rows, ending with a WS row. 37 sts.

Bind/cast off 4 sts at beg of next 2 rows.

Bind/cast off rem 29 sts.

FINISHING

PRESS as described on page 136.

Join right shoulder seam using backstitch, or mattress stitch if preferred.

Neckband

With RS facing and using size 2 (2³/₄mm) needles, pick up and knit 25 (25: 25: 27: 27) sts down left side of front neck, 21 (23: 23: 23: 23) sts from front, 25 (25: 25: 27: 27) sts up right side of front neck, then 49 (51: 51: 53: 53) sts from back.

120 (124: 124: 130: 130) sts.

Work in garter st for 2 rows, ending with a RS row.

Change to size 3 (3¹/₄mm) needles.

Row 3 (eyelet row) (WS): K1, *yo, K2tog, rep from * to last st, K1.

Change to size 2 (2³/₄mm) needles.

Work in garter st for 3 rows.

Bind/cast off knitwise (on WS).

See page 136 for finishing instructions, setting in sleeves using the set-in method. Thread ribbon through eyelet rows of sleeves and neckband, joining ends on inside and ensuring ribbon around neckband is long enough to go over head.

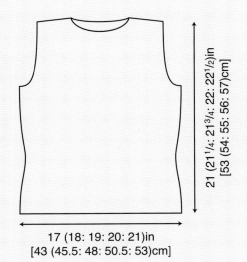

17 (18: 19: 20: 21)in
[43 (45.5: 48: 50.5: 53)cm]

21 (21¹/₄: 21³/₄: 22: 22¹/₂)in
[53 (54: 55: 56: 57)cm]

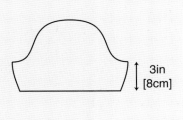

3in
[8cm]

DEMI
KIM HARGREAVES

The rugged Aran-inspired style of this knit is made
delightful by the shoulder fastening and the lacy collar
peeping out beneath the neckline. The cloche hat makes
the whole look both playful and original.

DEMI
KIM HARGREAVES

YARN AND SIZES

	XS	S	M	L	XL	
To fit bust	32	34	36	38	40	in
	81	86	91	97	102	cm

Rowan Yorkshire Tweed Aran

	6	6	7	7	7	x 100g

Use black (no. 414) or desired color

NEEDLES

1 pair size 6 (4mm) needles
1 pair size 7 (4¹/2mm) needles
1 pair size 8 (5mm) needles
Cable needle

BUTTONS—4 buttons (Rowan 00339)

GAUGE/TENSION

16 sts and 23 rows to 4in/10cm measured over
St st using size 8 (5mm) needles.

SPECIAL ABBREVIATIONS

Cr2R = slip next st onto cable needle and leave
at back of work, K1 tbl, then P1 from cable
needle.

Cr2L = slip next st onto cable needle and leave
at front of work, P1, then K1 tbl from cable
needle.

Cr3R = slip next st onto cable needle and leave
at back of work, (K1 tbl) twice, then P1 from
cable needle.

Cr3L = slip next 2 sts onto cable needle and
leave at front of work, P1, then (K1 tbl) twice
from cable needle.

C3B = slip next st onto cable needle and leave
at back of work, (K1 tbl) twice, then K1 tbl
from cable needle.

C3F = slip next 2 sts onto cable needle and
leave at front of work, K1 tbl, then (K1 tbl)
twice from cable needle.

MB (make bobble) = (K1, P1, K1, P1, K1) all
into next st, turn, P5, turn, lift 2nd, 3rd, 4th
then 5th st over first st and then K rem st tbl.

BACK

Cast on 91 (95: 99: 103: 107) sts using size 7
(4¹/2mm) needles.

Starting and ending rows as indicated, work in
patt foll chart for body as foll:

Work 18 rows, ending with a WS row.

Change to size 8 (5mm) needles.

Work 2 rows, ending after chart row 20.

Now repeating chart rows 21 to 44 **only** over
center sts and chart rows 21 to 40 **only** over
side sts, cont foll chart as foll:

Work 2 rows.

Dec 1 st at each end of next and every foll 4th
row until 83 (87: 91: 95: 99) sts rem.

Work 15 rows, ending with a WS row.

Inc 1 st at each end of next and every foll 8th
row until there are 91 (95: 99: 103: 107) sts,
taking inc sts into patt.

Work even/straight until back measures 14
(14¹/2: 14³/4: 15: 15)in/36 (37: 37: 38: 38)cm,
ending with a WS row.

Shape armholes

Keeping patt correct, bind/cast off 5 sts at beg
of next 2 rows. 81 (85: 89: 93: 97) sts.

Dec 1 st at each end of next 5 (5: 7: 7: 9) rows,
then on foll 3 (4: 4: 5: 5) alt rows.

65 (67: 67: 69: 69) sts.

Work even/straight until armhole measures 8
(8: 8¹/4: 8¹/4: 8³/4)in/20 (20: 21: 21: 22)cm,
ending with a WS row.

Shape shoulders and back neck

Bind/cast off 5 sts at beg of next 2 rows.
55 (57: 57: 59: 59) sts.

Next row (RS): Bind/cast off 5 sts, patt until
there are 10 sts on right needle and turn,
leaving rem sts on a holder.

Work each side of neck separately.

Bind/cast off 4 sts at beg of next row.

Bind/cast off rem 6 sts.

With RS facing, rejoin yarn to rem sts,
bind/cast off center 25 (27: 27: 29: 29) sts,
patt to end.

Complete to match first side, reversing shapings.

FRONT

Work as given for back until 14 rows less have
been worked than on back to start of shoulder
shaping, ending with a WS row.

Shape neck

Next row (RS): Patt 23 sts and turn, leaving
rem sts on a holder.

Work each side of neck separately.

Dec 1 st at neck edge of next 3 rows, ending
with a WS row. 20 sts.

Make a note of exactly which patt row has
just been completed and where in patt these sts
sit—you will need this for shoulder section.

Bind/cast off.

With RS facing, rejoin yarn to rem sts, bind/cast
off center 19 (21: 21: 23: 23) sts, patt to end.
23 sts.

Dec 1 st at neck edge on next 5 rows, then on
foll 2 alt rows. 16 sts.

Work 5 rows, ending with a RS row.

Shape shoulder

Bind/cast off 5 sts at beg of next and foll alt row.

Work 1 row.

Bind/cast off rem 6 sts.

Left front shoulder section

Cast on 20 sts using size 8 (5mm) needles.

Starting at exactly the point in patt and across
row as where left shoulder was bound-off/cast-
off, cont in patt as foll:

Dec 1 st at neck edge (end of first row) of next 2
rows, then on foll 2 alt rows.

16 sts.

Work 4 rows, ending with a WS row.

Shape shoulder

Bind/cast off 5 sts at beg of next and foll alt row.

Work 1 row.

Bind/cast off rem 6 sts.

SLEEVES (both alike)

Cast on 61 (61: 63: 63: 65) sts using size 7
(4¹/2mm) needles.

Row 1 (RS): P1 (1: 0: 0: 1), (K1 tbl, P1) 6 (6: 7:
7: 7) times, (K1 tbl) twice, P2, (K1 tbl, P1) 13

Body chart

20 row patt rep

24 row patt rep

20 row patt rep

44

40

30

20

10

x small
small
medium
large
x large

x small
small
medium
large
x large

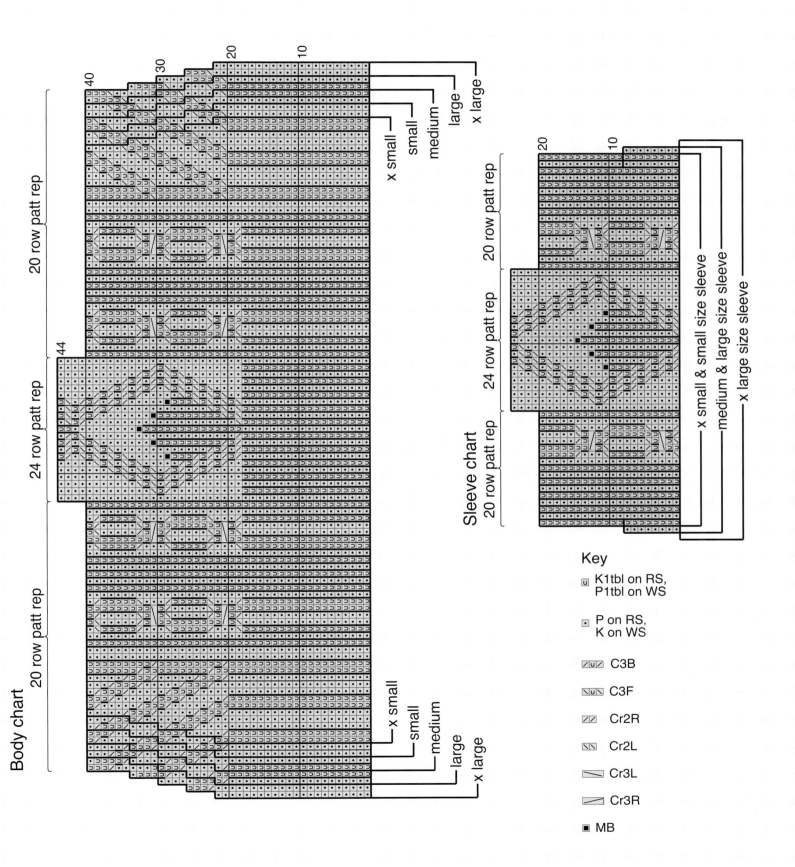

Sleeve chart

20 row patt rep

24 row patt rep

20 row patt rep

20

10

x small & small size sleeve

medium & large size sleeve

x large size sleeve

Key

⊍ K1tbl on RS,
P1tbl on WS

• P on RS,
K on WS

C3B

C3F

Cr2R

Cr2L

Cr3L

Cr3R

■ MB

times, K1 tbl, P2, (K1 tbl) twice, (P1, K1 tbl) 6 (6: 7: 7: 7) times, P1 (1: 0: 0: 1).

Row 2: K1 (1: 0: 0: 1), (P1 tbl, K1) 6 (6: 7: 7: 7) times, (P1 tbl) twice, K2, (P1 tbl, K1) 13 times, P1 tbl, K2, (P1 tbl) twice, (K1, P1 tbl) 6 (6: 7: 7: 7) times, K1 (1: 0: 0: 1).

These 2 rows form rib.

Cont in rib, dec 1 st at each end of 9th and every foll 8th row until 55 (55: 57: 57: 59) sts rem.

Work 7 rows, ending with a WS row.

(34 rows of rib completed.)

Change to size 8 (5mm) needles.

Starting and ending rows as indicated, repeating chart rows 1 to 24 **only** over center sts and chart rows 1 to 20 **only** over side sts, work in patt foll chart for sleeve as foll:

Dec 1 st at each end of next and foll 8th row. 51 (51: 53: 53: 55) sts.

Work 13 rows, ending with a WS row.

Inc 1 st at each end of next and every foll 6th row to 57 (57: 57: 57: 59) sts, then on every foll 8th row until there are 63 (63: 65: 65: 67) sts, taking inc sts into rib.

Work even/straight until sleeve measures 17½ (17½: 18: 18: 18)in/45 (45: 46: 46: 46)cm, ending with a WS row.

Shape sleeve cap

Keeping patt correct, bind/cast off 5 sts at beg of next 2 rows.

53 (53: 55: 55: 57) sts.

Dec 1 st at each end of next 3 rows, then on foll alt row, then on every foll 4th row until 37 (37: 39: 39: 41) sts rem.

Work 1 row, ending with a WS row.

Dec 1 st at each end of next and every foll alt row to 33 sts, then on foll 5 rows, ending with a WS row.

Bind/cast off rem 23 sts.

FINISHING

PRESS as described on page 136.

Join both shoulder seams using backstitch, or mattress stitch if preferred.

Left front shoulder buttonhole band

Cast on 9 sts using size 6 (4mm) needles.

Row 1 (RS): K1, (K1 tbl, P1) 3 times, K1 tbl, K1.

Row 2: K1, (P1 tbl, K1) 4 times.

These 2 rows form rib.

Work in rib for 8 rows more, ending with a WS row.

Row 11 (buttonhole row) (RS): Rib 3, work 2 tog, yo (to make a buttonhole), rib 4.

Work 7 rows.

Rep last 8 rows once more, ending with a WS row. Do NOT break yarn.

Neckband

With RS facing and using size 6 (4mm) needles, work across 9 sts of buttonhole band as foll: rib 3, work 2 tog, yo (to make 3rd buttonhole), rib 4, pick up and knit 4 sts down left side of neck, 13 (15: 15: 17: 17) sts from front, 16 sts up right side of neck, 26 (28: 28: 30: 30) sts from back, then 13 sts down left side of neck to cast-on edge of left front shoulder section. 81 (85: 85: 89: 89) sts.

Row 1 (WS): K1, *P1 tbl, K1, rep from * to end.

Row 2: K1, *K1 tbl, P1, rep from * to last 2 sts, K1 tbl, K1.

These 2 rows form rib.

Cont in rib for 5 rows more.

Row 8 (RS): rib 3, work 2 tog, yo (to make 4th buttonhole), rib to end.

Work in rib for 3 rows more.

Bind/cast off in rib.

Slip stitch edge of left front shoulder buttonhole band to bound-off/cast-off edge of left front shoulder.

Lay buttonhole band over left front shoulder section so that buttonhole band seam matches cast-on edge and sew together at armhole edge.

See page 136 for finishing instructions, setting in sleeves using the set-in method.

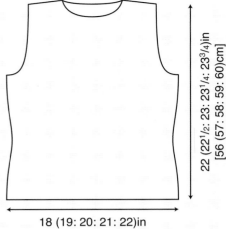

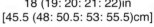

22 (22½: 23: 23¼: 23¾)in [56 (57: 58: 59: 60)cm]

18 (19: 20: 21: 22)in [45.5 (48: 50.5: 53: 55.5)cm]

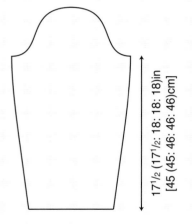

17½ (17½: 18: 18: 18)in [45 (45: 46: 46: 46)cm]

TOUSCON SCAPE
BRANDON MABLY

This jacket is a celebration of rich, dark colors, drawn in broad strokes to make merging stripes. The colors remind us of the palettes of twentieth-century European artists such as Pierre Bonnard and Toulouse-Lautrec.

TOUSCON SCAPE
BRANDON MABLY

YARN AND SIZES

	XS	S	M	L	XL	
To fit bust	32	34	36	38	40	in
	81	6	91	97	102	cm

Rowan Yorkshire Tweed Chunky, Aran, DK

A = Chunky—blue (no. 555) or desired color

	3	4	4	4	4	x 100g

B = *Aran—dark aqua (no. 415) or desired color

	3	3	3	3	3	x 100g

C = *DK—light green (no. 348) or desired color

	3	3	3	3	3	x 50g

D = *Aran—camel (no. 413) or desired color

	3	3	3	3	3	x 100g

E = Chunky—gray-green (no. 550) or desired color

	2	2	2	2	2	x 100g

F = Chunky—terra cotta (no. 553) or desired color

	2	2	2	2	2	x 100g

G = *DK—red (no. 343) or desired color

	2	2	2	2	2	x 50g

H = Chunky—ecru (no. 551) or desired color

	2	2	2	2	2	x 100g

*Use TWO STRANDS of Yorkshire Tweed Aran and Yorkshire Tweed DK throughout.

NEEDLES

1 pair size 10½ (7mm) needles
1 pair size 11 (8mm) needles

BUTTONS—5 buttons (Rowan 00340)

GAUGE/TENSION

12 sts and 16 rows to 4in/10cm measured over patterned St st using size 11 (8mm) needles.

BACK

Cast on 69 (71: 75: 77: 81) sts using size 10½ (7mm) needles and yarn A.
Beg with a K row, work in St st for 9 rows, ending with a RS row.
Row 10: Knit (to form fold line).
Change to size 11 (8mm) needles.
Starting and ending rows as indicated and using the **intarsia** technique, cont in patt from chart, which is worked entirely in St st beg with a K row, as foll:
Dec 1 st at each end of 15th and every foll 12th row until 63 (65: 69: 71: 75) sts rem.
Work 17 rows, ending with a WS row.
Inc 1 st at each end of next and every foll 8th row until there are 69 (71: 75: 77: 81) sts, taking inc sts into patt.
Work even/straight until chart row 82 (84: 84: 86: 86) has been completed, ending with a WS row. Back should measure 20 (20½: 20½: 21: 21¼)in/51 (53: 53: 54: 54)cm from fold line.

Shape armholes

Keeping patt correct, bind/cast off 5 sts at beg of next 2 rows.
59 (61: 65: 67: 71) sts.
Dec 1 st at each end of next 3 (3: 5: 5: 7) rows, then on foll 2 alt rows, then on foll 4th row.
47 (49: 49: 51: 51) sts.
Work even/straight until chart row 120 (122: 124: 126: 128) has been completed, ending with a WS row. Armhole should measure 9½ (9½: 10: 10: 10¼)in/24 (24: 25: 25: 26)cm.

Shape shoulders and back neck

Next row (RS): Bind/cast off 7 sts, patt until there are 10 sts on right needle and turn, leaving rem sts on a holder.
Work each side of neck separately.
Bind/cast off 3 sts at beg of next row.
Bind/cast off rem 7 sts.
With RS facing, rejoin yarns to rem sts, bind/cast off center 13 (15: 15: 17: 17) sts, patt to end.
Complete to match first side, reversing shapings.

LEFT FRONT

Cast on 36 (37: 39: 40: 42) sts using size 10½ (7mm) needles and yarn A.
Beg with a K row, work in St st for 9 rows, ending with a RS row.
Row 10: Knit (to form fold line).
Change to size 11 (8mm) needles.
Starting and ending rows as indicated, cont in patt from chart as foll:
Dec 1 st at beg of 15th and every foll 12th row until 33 (34: 36: 37: 39) sts rem.
Work 17 rows, ending with a WS row.
Inc 1 st at beg of next and every foll 8th row until there are 36 (37: 39: 40: 42) sts, taking inc sts into patt.
Work even/straight until left front matches back to beg of armhole shaping, ending with a WS row.

Shape armhole

Keeping patt correct, bind/cast off 5 sts at beg of next row.
31 (32: 34: 35: 37) sts.
Work 1 row.
Dec 1 st at armhole edge of next 3 (3: 5: 5: 7) rows, then on foll 2 alt rows, then on foll 4th row.
25 (26: 26: 27: 27) sts.
Work even/straight until chart row 109 (111: 113: 115: 117) has been completed, ending with a RS row.

Shape neck

Keeping patt correct, bind/cast off 6 (7: 7: 8: 8) sts at beg of next row. 19 sts.
Dec 1 st at neck edge on next 3 rows, then on foll 2 alt rows. 14 sts.
Work 3 rows, ending with chart row 120 (122: 124: 126: 128) and a WS row.

Shape shoulder

Bind/cast off 7 sts at beg of next row.
Work 1 row.
Bind/cast off rem 7 sts.

RIGHT FRONT

Cast on 36 (37: 39: 40: 42) sts using size 10½ (7mm) needles and yarn A.
Beg with a K row, work in St st for 9 rows, ending with a RS row.
Row 10: Knit (to form fold line).
Change to size 11 (8mm) needles.
Starting and ending rows as indicated, cont in patt from chart as foll:

Dec 1 st at end of 15th and foll 0 (12th: 12th: 12th: 12th) row.

35 (35: 37: 38: 40) sts.

Work 11 (1: 3: 5: 7) rows, ending with a WS row.

Next row (buttonhole row) (RS): Patt 2 sts, bind/cast off 2 sts (to make a buttonhole—cast on 2 sts over these bound-off/cast-off sts on next row), patt to last 2 (0: 0: 0: 0) sts, (work 2 tog) 1 (0: 0: 0: 0) times.

34 (35: 37: 38: 40) sts.

Dec 1 st at end of 12th (10th: 8th: 6th: 4th) row. 33 (34: 36: 37: 39) sts.

Making 4 buttonholes more on every foll 20th row from previous buttonhole, complete to match left front, reversing shapings.

SLEEVES (both alike)

Cast on 33 (33: 33: 35: 35) sts using size 10½ (7mm) needles and yarn A.

Beg with a K row, work in St st for 9 rows, ending with a RS row.

Row 10: Knit (to form fold line).

Change to size 11 (8mm) needles.

Starting and ending rows as indicated, cont in patt from chart as foll:

Inc 1 st at each end of 11th and every foll 10th (10th: 8th: 10th: 8th) row to 39 (39: 37: 39: 39) sts, then on every foll 12th (12th: 10th: 12th: 10th) row until there are 45 (45: 47: 47: 49) sts, taking inc sts into patt.

Work even/straight until chart row 74 (74: 76: 76: 76) has been completed, ending with a WS row. Sleeve should measure 18 (18: 19: 19: 19)in/46 (46: 48: 48: 48)cm from fold line.

Shape sleeve cap

Keeping patt correct, bind/cast off 5 sts at beg of next 2 rows. 35 (35: 37: 37: 39) sts.

Dec 1 st at each end of next 3 rows, then on foll alt row, then on every foll 4th row until 21 (21: 23: 23: 25) sts rem.

Work 1 row, ending with a WS row.

Dec 1 st at each end of next and every foll alt row

to 15 sts, then on foll row, end with a WS row. Bind/cast off rem 13 sts.

FINISHING

PRESS as described on page 136.

Join both shoulder seams using backstitch, or mattress stitch if preferred.

Front bands (both alike)

With RS facing, using size 10½ (7mm) needles and yarn A, pick up and knit 81 (83: 84: 86: 87) sts along front opening edge, between fold line row and neck shaping.

Work in garter st (K every row) for 2 rows.

Bind/cast off knitwise (on WS).

Collar

With RS facing, using size 10½ (7mm) needles and yarn A, starting and ending at front opening edges, pick up and knit 19 (20: 20: 21: 21) sts up right side of neck, 21 (23: 23: 25: 25) sts from back, then 19 (20: 20: 21: 21) sts down left side of neck.

59 (63: 63: 67: 67) sts.

Work in garter st for 28 rows.

Bind/cast off knitwise.

See page 136 for finishing instructions, setting in sleeves using the set-in method. Fold first 9 rows of sleeves and body to inside along fold line rows and stitch in place.

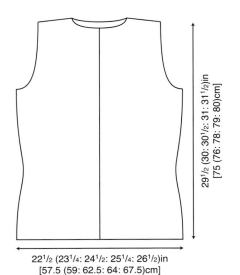

22½ (23¼: 24½: 25¼: 26½)in
[57.5 (59: 62.5: 64: 67.5)cm]

29½ (30: 30½: 31: 31½)in
[75 (76: 78: 79: 80)cm]

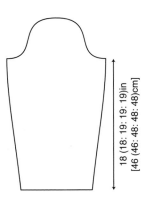

18 (18: 19: 19: 19)in
[46 (46: 48: 48: 48)cm]

TOUSCON SCAPE
BRANDON MABLY

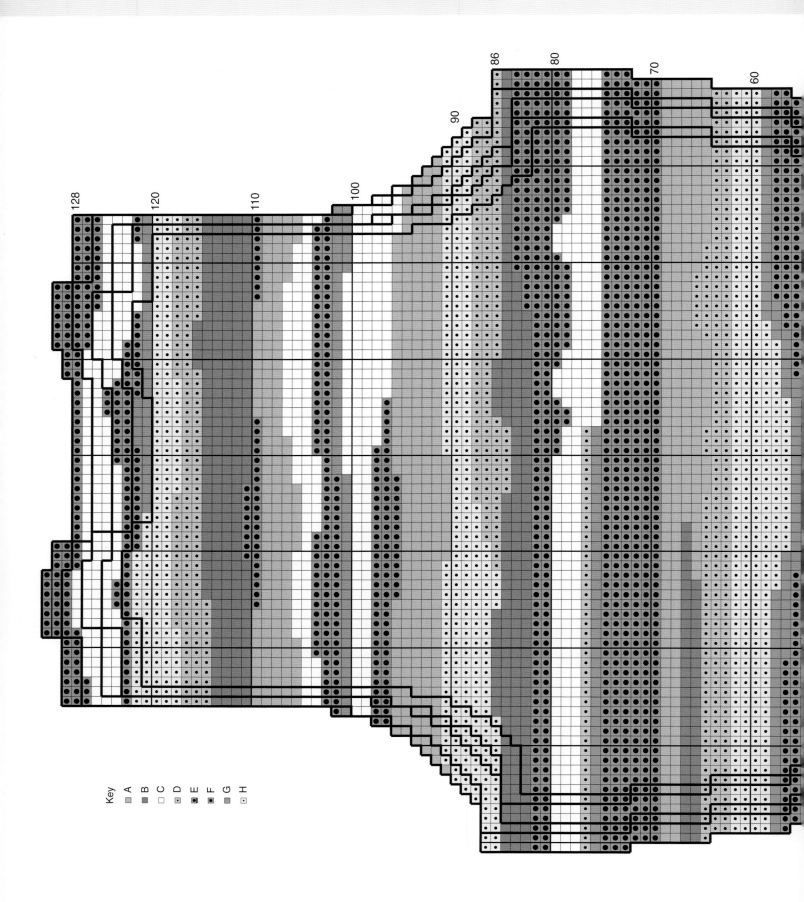

Key A B C D E F G H

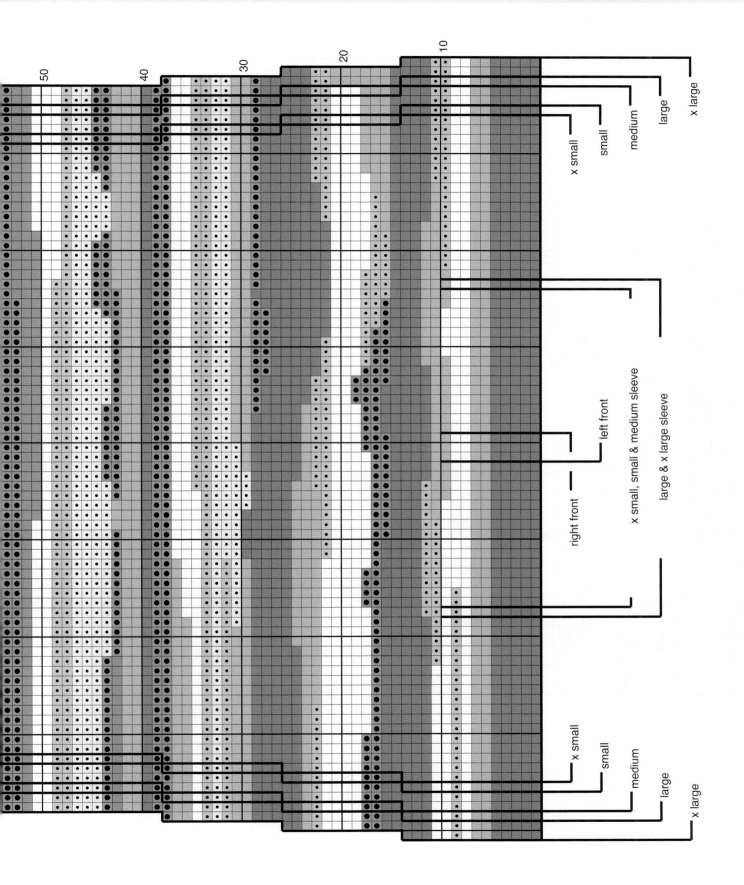

50

40

30

20

10

x small
small
medium
large
x large

left front

x small, small & medium sleeve

large & x large sleeve

right front

x small
small
medium
large
x large

CHARLOT
MARTIN STOREY

At once sweet and sophisticated, this cardigan has a delicacy, created by the embroidered decoration on the textured background, with the yarn giving a subtle sheen. Here, the red polka-dot dress perfectly brings out the red used for the flowers.

YARN AND SIZES

	XS	S	M	L	XL	
To fit bust	32	34	36	38	40	in
	81	86	91	97	102	cm

Rowan 4 ply Soft

A = lilac (no. 375) or desired MC

	10	10	11	11	12	x 50g

B = light green (no. 379) or desired 1st CC

	1	1	1	1	1	x 50g

C = red (no. 374) or desired 2nd CC

	1	1	1	1	1	x 50g

D = light turquoise (no. 373) or desired 3rd CC

	1	1	1	1	1	x 50g

E = pink (no. 377) or desired 4th CC

	1	1	1	1	1	x 50g

NEEDLES

1 pair size 2 (2³/₄mm) needles
1 pair size 3 (3¹/₄mm) needles
Cable needle

BUTTONS—8 buttons (Rowan 00322)

GAUGE/TENSION

28 sts and 36 rows to 4in/10cm measured over St st using size 3 (3¹/₄mm) needles.

SPECIAL ABBREVIATIONS

Cr2R = slip next st onto cable needle and leave at back of work, K1 tbl, then P1 from cable needle.
Cr2L = slip next st onto cable needle and leave at front of work, P1, then K1 tbl from cable needle.
MB (make bobble) = (K1, P1, K1) all into next st, turn, P3, turn, K3, turn, P3, turn, sl 1, K2tog, psso.

BACK

Cast on 107 (113: 121: 127: 135) sts using size 2 (2³/₄mm) needles and yarn A.
Row 1 (RS): K1 (0: 2: 0: 0), P3 (1: 3: 2: 0), *K3, P3, rep from * to last 1 (4: 2: 5: 3) sts,

CHARLOT
MARTIN STOREY

K1 (3: 2: 3: 3), P0 (1: 0: 2: 0).

Row 2: P1 (0: 2: 0: 0), K3 (1: 3: 2: 0), *P3, K3, rep from * to last 1 (4: 2: 5: 3) sts, P1 (3: 2: 3: 3), K0 (1: 0: 2: 0).

These 2 rows form rib.

Cont in rib for 3¹/₂in/9cm, ending with a RS row.

Next row (WS): Inc in first st, rib 26 (29: 33: 36: 40), M1, (rib 1, M1) twice, rib 21, M1, (rib 1, M1) twice, rib 3, M1, (rib 1, M1) twice, rib 21, M1, (rib 1, M1) twice, rib to last st, inc in last st.

121 (127: 135: 141: 149) sts.

Change to size 3 (3¹/₄mm) needles.

Starting and ending rows as indicated, working chart rows 1 and 2 once only and then repeating chart rows 3 to 38 throughout, cont in patt from chart for body as foll:

Inc 1 st at each end of 9th and every foll 8th row until there are 135 (141: 149: 155: 163) sts, taking inc sts into rev St st.

Work even/straight until back measures 11 (11¹/₄: 11¹/₄: 11³/₄: 12)in/28 (29: 29: 30: 30)cm, ending with a WS row.

Shape armholes

Keeping patt correct, bind/cast off 5 (6: 6: 7: 7) sts at beg of next 2 rows.

125 (129: 137: 141: 149) sts.

Dec 1 st at each end of next 5 (5: 7: 7: 9) rows, then on foll 3 (4: 4: 5: 5) alt rows, then on every foll 4th row until 105 (107: 111: 113: 117) sts.

Work even/straight until armhole measures 8 (8: 8¹/₄: 8¹/₄: 8¹/₂)in/20 (20: 21: 21: 22)cm, ending with a WS row.

Shape shoulders and back neck

Bind/cast off 9 (9: 10: 10: 11) sts at beg of next 2 rows.

87 (89: 91: 93: 95) sts.

Next row (RS): Bind/cast off 9 (9: 10: 10: 11) sts, patt until there are 14 sts on right needle and turn, leaving rem sts on a holder.

Work each side of neck separately.

Bind/cast off 4 sts at beg of next row.

Bind/cast off rem 10 sts.

With RS facing, rejoin yarn to rem sts, bind/cast off center 41 (43: 43: 45: 45) sts dec 6 sts even/straightly, patt to end.

Complete to match first side, reversing shapings.

LEFT FRONT

Cast on 54 (57: 61: 64: 68) sts using size 2 (2³/₄mm) needles and yarn A.

Row 1 (RS): K1 (0: 2: 0: 0), P3 (1: 3: 2: 0), *K3, P3, rep from * to last 2 sts, K2.

Row 2: P2, K3, *P3, K3, rep from * to last 1 (4: 2: 5: 3) sts, P1 (3: 2: 3: 3), K0 (1: 0: 2: 0).

These 2 rows form rib.

Cont in rib for 3¹/₂in/9cm, ending with RS row.

Next row (WS): Rib 2, M1, (rib 1, M1) twice, rib 21, M1, (rib 1, M1) twice, rib to last st, inc in last st. 61 (64: 68: 71: 75) sts.

Change to size 3 (3¹/₄mm) needles.

Starting and ending rows as indicated, cont in patt from chart for body as foll:

Inc 1 st at beg of 9th and every foll 8th row until there are 68 (71: 75: 78: 82) sts.

Work even/straight until left front matches back to beg of armhole shaping, ending with a WS row.

Shape armhole

Keeping patt correct, bind/cast off 5 (6: 6: 7: 7) sts at beg of next row. 63 (65: 69: 71: 75) sts.

Work 1 row.

Dec 1 st at armhole edge of next 5 (5: 7: 7: 9) rows, then on foll 3 (4: 4: 5: 5) alt rows, then on every foll 4th row until 53 (54: 56: 57: 59) sts.

Work even/straight until 21 (21: 21: 23: 23) rows less have been worked than on back to start of shoulder shaping, ending with a RS row.

Shape neck

Keeping patt correct, bind/cast off 8 (9: 9: 9: 9) sts at beg of next row, then 5 sts at beg of foll alt row. 40 (40: 42: 43: 45) sts.

Dec 1 st at neck edge on next 7 rows, then on foll 5 (5: 5: 6: 6) alt rows.

28 (28: 30: 30: 32) sts.

Work 1 row, ending with a WS row.

Shape shoulder

Bind/cast off 9 (9: 10: 10: 11) sts at beg of next and foll alt row.

Work 1 row. Bind/cast off rem 10 sts.

RIGHT FRONT

Cast on 54 (57: 61: 64: 68) sts using size 2 (2³/₄mm) needles and yarn A.

Row 1 (RS): K2, P3, *K3, P3, rep from * to last 1 (4: 2: 5: 3) sts, K1 (3: 2: 3: 3), P0 (1: 0: 2: 0).

Row 2: P1 (0: 2: 0: 0), K3 (1: 3: 2: 0), *P3, K3, rep from * to last 2 sts, P2.

These 2 rows form rib.

Cont in rib for 3¹/₂in/9cm, ending with a RS row.

Next row (WS): Inc in first st, rib 26 (29: 33: 36: 40), M1, (rib 1, M1) twice, rib 21, M1, (rib 1, M1) twice, rib 2. 61 (64: 68: 71: 75) sts.

Change to size 3 (3¹/₄mm) needles.

Starting and ending rows as indicated, cont in patt from chart for body as foll:

Inc 1 st at end of 9th and every foll 8th row until there are 68 (71: 75: 78: 82) sts.

Complete to match left front, reversing shapings.

SLEEVES (both alike)

Cast on 63 (63: 65: 67: 67) sts using size 2 (2³/₄mm) needles and yarn A.

Row 1 (RS): P0 (0: 1: 2: 2), *K3, P3, rep from * to last 3 (3: 4: 5: 5) sts, K3, P0 (0: 1: 2: 2).

Row 2: K0 (0: 1: 2: 2), *P3, K3, rep from * to last 3 (3: 4: 5: 5) sts, P3, K0 (0: 1: 2: 2).

These 2 rows form rib.

Cont in rib for 3¹/₂in/9cm, ending with a RS row.

Next row (WS): Inc in first st, rib 27 (27: 28: 29: 29), M1, (rib 1, M1) twice, rib 3, M1, (rib 1, M1) twice, rib to last st, inc in last st.

71 (71: 73: 75: 75) sts.

Change to size 3 (3¹/₄mm) needles.

Starting and ending rows as indicated, working chart rows 1 and 2 once only and then

112

repeating chart rows 3 to 38 throughout, cont in patt from chart for sleeve as foll:

Inc 1 st at each end of 7th (5th: 5th: 5th: 5th) and every foll 8th (6th: 6th: 6th: 6th) row to 93 (75: 81: 83: 99) sts, then on every foll 10th (8th: 8th: 8th: 8th) row until there are 97 (99: 103: 105: 109) sts, taking inc sts into rev St st.

Work even/straight until sleeve measures 17$\frac{1}{2}$ (17$\frac{1}{2}$: 17$\frac{3}{4}$: 17$\frac{3}{4}$: 17$\frac{3}{4}$)in/44 (44: 45: 45: 45)cm, ending with a WS row.

Shape sleeve cap

Keeping patt correct, bind/cast off 5 (6: 6: 7: 7) sts at beg of next 2 rows.

87 (87: 91: 91: 95) sts.

Dec 1 st at each end of next 5 rows, then on foll 4 alt rows, then on every foll 4th row until 59 (59: 63: 63: 67) sts rem.

Work 1 row, ending with a WS row.

Dec 1 st at each end of next and every foll alt row to 47 sts, then on foll 7 rows, end with a WS row.

Bind/cast off rem 33 sts, dec 6 sts evenly.

FINISHING

PRESS as described on page 136.

Join both shoulder seams using backstitch, or mattress stitch if preferred.

Neckband

With RS facing, using size 2 (2$\frac{3}{4}$mm) needles and yarn A, starting and ending at front opening edges, pick up and knit 33 (34: 34: 37: 37) sts up right side of neck, 47 (51: 51: 51: 51) sts from back, then 33 (34: 34: 37: 37) sts down left side of neck. 113 (119: 119: 125: 125) sts.

Body chart

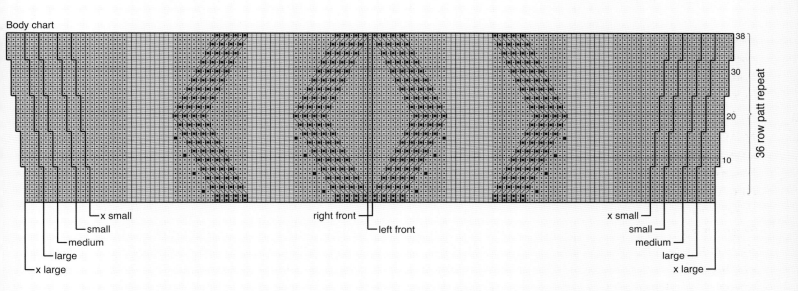

38
30
20
10

36 row patt repeat

x small
small
medium
large
x large

right front
left front

x small
small
medium
large
x large

Key

☐ K on RS, P on WS

⊡ P on RS, K on WS

⊙ K1 tbl on RS, P1 tbl on WS

■ MB

▨ Cr2R

◩ Cr2L

Sleeve chart

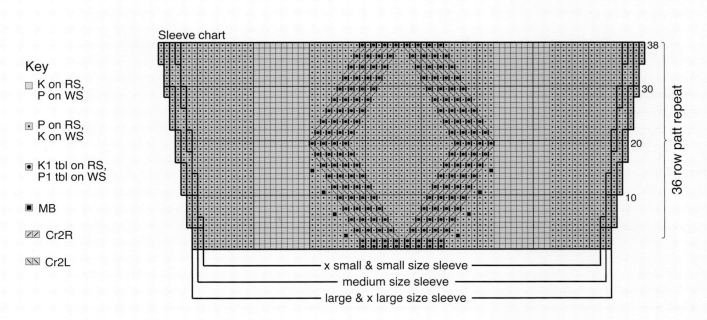

38
30
20
10

36 row patt repeat

x small & small size sleeve
medium size sleeve
large & x large size sleeve

Row 1 (WS): K1, *P3, K3, rep from * to last 4 sts, P3, K1.

Row 2: K4, *P3, K3, rep from * to last st, K1.

These 2 rows form rib. Work in rib for 3 rows more.

Bind/cast off in rib.

Button band

With RS facing, using size 2 (2³/4mm) needles and yarn A, pick up and knit 131 (131: 137: 137: 137) sts down left front opening edge, between top of neckband and cast-on edge.

Work in rib as given for neckband for 5 rows.

Bind/cast off in rib.

Buttonhole band

With RS facing, using size 2 (2³/4mm) needles and yarn A, pick up and knit 131 (131: 137: 137: 137) sts up right front opening edge, between cast-on edge and top of neckband.

Work in rib as given for neckband for 3 rows.

Row 4 (RS): Rib 2 (2: 3: 3: 3), work 2 tog, yo (to make a buttonhole), (rib 10, work 2 tog, yo) twice, *rib 18 (18: 19: 19: 19), work 2 tog, yo, rep from * to last 3 sts, rib 3.

Work in rib for 1 row more.

Bind/cast off in rib.

Embroidery

Following diagram, embroider design onto fronts.

See page 136 for finishing instructions, setting in sleeves using the set-in method.

Embroidery Diagram

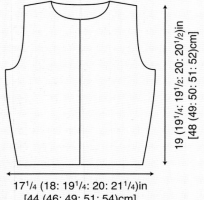

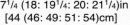

17¹/4 (18: 19¹/4: 20: 21¹/4)in
[44 (46: 49: 51: 54)cm]

19 (19¹/4: 19¹/2: 20: 20¹/2)in [48 (49: 50: 51: 52)cm]

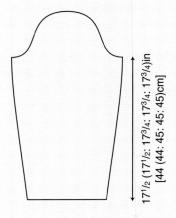

17¹/2 (17¹/2: 17³/4: 17³/4: 17³/4)in [44 (44: 45: 45: 45)cm]

RIVA
KIM HARGREAVES

The long lines of this coat, worn with a soft blouse, make it an elegant,
flattering shape that skims the body. Here it's set off by a large corsage that picks
up the color of the skirt.

YARN AND SIZES

	XS	S	M	L	XL	
To fit bust	32	34	36	38	40	in
	81	86	91	97	102	cm

Rowan Yorkshire Tweed Chunky

| | 11 | 11 | 12 | 13 | 13 | x 100g |

Use dark brown (no. 554) or desired color
For corsage, small amount of Yorkshire Tweed
4 ply in each of four shades and small amount
of Kid Silk Haze

NEEDLES

1 pair size 10½ (7mm) needles
1 pair size 11 (8mm) needles
1 pair size 3 (3¼mm) needles

GAUGE/TENSION

12 sts and 16 rows to 4in/10cm measured over
seed/moss stitch using size 11 (8mm) needles.

BACK

Cast on 71 (73: 77: 79: 83) sts using size 11
(8mm) needles.
Row 1 (RS): K1, *P1, K1, rep from * to end.
Row 2: As row 1.
These 2 rows form seed/moss st.
Cont in seed/moss st until back measures 24¾
(25¼: 25¼: 25½: 25½)in/63 (64: 64: 65:
65)cm, ending with a WS row.

Shape armholes

Keeping seed/moss st correct, bind/cast off 3 sts
at beg of next 2 rows.
65 (67: 71: 73: 77) sts.
Dec 1 st at each end of next 5 (5: 7: 7: 9) rows,
then on foll alt row, then on foll 4th row.
51 (53: 53: 55: 55) sts.
Work even/straight until armhole measures 8¾
(8¾: 9: 9: 9½)in/22 (22: 23: 23: 24)cm, ending
with a WS row.

Shape shoulders and back neck

Bind/cast off 6 sts at beg of next 2 rows.
39 (41: 41: 43: 43) sts.
Next row (RS): Bind/cast off 6 sts, seed/moss

st until there are 9 sts on right needle and turn,
leaving rem sts on a holder.
Work each side of neck separately.
Bind/cast off 4 sts at beg of next row.
Bind/cast off rem 5 sts.
With RS facing, rejoin yarn to rem sts,
bind/cast off center 9 (11: 11: 13: 13) sts,
seed/moss st to end.
Complete to match first side, reversing
shapings.

LEFT FRONT

Cast on 36 (37: 39: 40: 42) sts using size 11
(8mm) needles.
Row 1 (RS): *K1, P1, rep from * to last 0 (1:
1: 0: 0) st, K0 (1: 1: 0: 0).
Row 2: K0 (1: 1: 0: 0), *P1, K1, rep from
* to end.
These 2 rows form seed/moss st.
Cont in seed/moss st until left front matches
back to beg of armhole shaping, ending with a
WS row.

Shape armhole

Keeping seed/moss st correct, bind/cast off 3
sts at beg of next row.
33 (34: 36: 37: 39) sts.
Work 1 row.
Dec 1 st at armhole edge of next 5 (5: 7: 7: 9)
rows, then on foll alt row, then on foll 4th row.
26 (27: 27: 28: 28) sts.
Work even/straight until 13 rows less have been
worked than on back to start of shoulder
shaping, ending with a RS row.

Shape neck

Next row (WS): Seed st 3 (4: 4: 5: 5) sts and
slip these sts onto a holder, seed/moss st to end.
23 sts.
Dec 1 st at neck edge on next 4 rows, then on
foll alt row, then on foll 4th row. 17 sts.
Work 2 rows, ending with a WS row.

Shape shoulder

Bind/cast off 6 sts at beg of next and foll alt
row.

Work 1 row.
Bind/cast off rem 5 sts.

RIGHT FRONT

Cast on 36 (37: 39: 40: 42) sts using size 11
(8mm) needles.
Row 1 (RS): K0 (1: 1: 0: 0), *P1, K1, rep from
* to end.
Row 2: *K1, P1, rep from * to last 0 (1: 1: 0:
0) st, K0 (1: 1: 0: 0).
These 2 rows form seed/moss st.
Complete to match left front, reversing shapings.

SLEEVES (both alike)

Cast on 35 (35: 35: 37: 37) sts using size 11
(8mm) needles.
Work in seed/moss st as given for back,
shaping sides by inc 1 st at each end of 17th
(17th: 15th: 17th: 17th) and every foll 16th
(16th: 14th: 16th: 14th) row to 41 (41: 39: 45:
41) sts, then on every foll 14th (14th: 12th: -:
12th) row until there are 43 (43: 45: -: 47) sts,
taking inc sts into seed/moss st.
Work even until sleeve measures 17 (17: 17½:
17½: 17½)in/44 (44: 45: 45: 45)cm, ending
with a WS row.

Shape sleeve cap

Keeping seed/moss st correct, bind/cast off 3
sts at beg of next 2 rows.
37 (37: 39: 39: 41) sts.
Dec 1 st at each end of next 3 rows, then on
foll alt row, then on every foll 4th row until
23 (23: 25: 25: 27) sts rem.
Work 1 row, ending with a WS row.
Dec 1 st at each end of next and every foll alt
row to 17 sts, then on foll row, ending with a
WS row.
Bind/cast off rem 15 sts.

FINISHING

PRESS as described on page 136.
Join both shoulder seams using backstitch, or
mattress stitch if preferred.

Neckband

With RS facing and using size 10¹/₂ (7mm)
needles, slip 3 (4: 4: 5: 5) sts left on right front
holder onto right needle, rejoin yarn and pick
up and knit 16 sts up right side of neck, 17 (19:
19: 21: 21) sts from back, and 16 sts down left
side of neck, then seed/moss st 3 (4: 4: 5: 5) sts
from left front holder.
55 (59: 59: 63: 63) sts.
Bind/cast off knitwise (on WS).
See page 136 for finishing instructions, setting
in sleeves using the set-in method.

CORSAGE
BACK SECTION

Using size 3 (3¹/₄mm) needles and first shade
of Yorkshire Tweed 4 ply, cast on 28 sts.
Beg with a K row and working in 2 row stripes
of first and second shades, cont in St st until
work is a perfect square.
Bind/cast off.

FRONT SECTION

Work as for back section but using third and
fourth shades of Yorkshire Tweed 4 ply.

CENTER SECTION

Cast on 6 sts using TWO STRANDS of Kid
Silk Haze held tog and size 3 (3¹/₄mm) needles.
Cont in rev St st, inc 1 st at end of next 6 rows.
12 sts. Dec 1 st at end of next 6 rows. 6 sts.
Bind/cast off.

FINISHING

Machine hot wash, then dry back and front
sections to shrink and felt them. Press.
From back section, cut a 3in/7.5cm diameter
circle, and from front section, cut a 2¹/₄in/6cm
diameter circle.
Run gathering threads around outer edge of
center section and pull tight so that center
section forms a soft, flat ball.
Fasten ends off securely.

Lay front section on back section, and run
gathering threads through both layers around
center point. Pull threads tight so that sections
form a rumpled flower shape and fasten ends
off securely. Position center section over these
gathering threads and sew all 3 sections
together at center.
If desired, attach a safety pin or brooch back to
back of corsage.

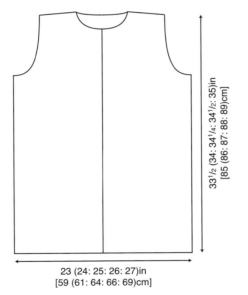

33¹/₂ (34: 34¹/₄: 34¹/₂: 35)in
[85 (86: 87: 88: 89)cm]

23 (24: 25: 26: 27)in
[59 (61: 64: 66: 69)cm]

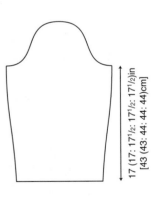

17 (17: 17¹/₂: 17¹/₂: 17¹/₂)in
[43 (43: 44: 44: 44)cm]

JARRETT
KIM HARGREAVES

This jacket, knitted up in a tweedy natural yarn and with shoulder patches, has a
real artisan feel. It's a look favored by intellectuals, painters, and writers striving to
rediscover nature and return to the simple life.

YARN AND SIZES

	S	M	L	XL	XXL	
To fit chest	38	40	42	44	46	in
	97	102	107	112	117	cm

Rowan Yorkshire Tweed DK

	13	14	15	16	16	x 50g

Use light brown (no. 353) or desired color

NEEDLES

1 pair size 3 (3¼mm) needles
1 pair size 5 (3¾mm) needles
1 pair size 6 (4mm) needles

BUTTONS—7 buttons (Rowan 00340)

GAUGE/TENSION

20 sts and 28 rows to 4in/10cm measured over
St st using size 6 (4mm) needles.

BACK

Cast on 113 (117: 123: 127: 133) sts using
size 5 (3¾mm) needles.
Row 1 (RS): K1, *P1, K1, rep from * to end.
Row 2: P1, *K1, P1, rep from * to end.
These 2 rows form rib.
Cont in rib for 24 rows more, ending with a
WS row.
Change to size 6 (4mm) needles.
Beg with a K row, cont in St st until back
measures 16¾ (17: 17½: 17½: 17¾)in/43 (43:
44: 44: 45)cm, ending with a WS row.
Shape armholes
Bind/cast off 5 (5: 6: 6: 7) sts at beg of next 2
rows. 103 (107: 111: 115: 119) sts.
Dec 1 st at each end of next 5 (7: 7: 9: 9) rows,
then on foll 2 (1: 2: 1: 2) alt rows, then on every
foll 4th row until 85 (87: 89: 91: 93) sts rem.
Work even/straight until armhole measures
8¾ (9: 9: 9½: 9½)in/22 (23: 23: 24: 24)cm,
ending with a WS row.
Shape shoulders and back neck
Bind/cast off 8 sts at beg of next 2 rows.
69 (71: 73: 75: 77) sts.

Next row (RS): Bind/cast off 8 sts, K until
there are 12 (12: 13: 13: 13) sts on right needle
and turn, leaving rem sts on a holder.
Work each side of neck separately.
Bind/cast off 4 sts at beg of next row.
Bind/cast off rem 8 (8: 9: 9: 9) sts.
With RS facing, rejoin yarn to rem sts, bind/
cast off center 29 (31: 31: 33: 35) sts, K to end.
Complete to match first side, reversing shapings.

LEFT FRONT

Cast on 64 (66: 68: 70: 74) sts using size 5
(3¾mm) needles.
Row 1 (RS): *K1, P1, rep from * to last
2 sts, K2.
Row 2: *K1, P1, rep from * to end.
These 2 rows form rib.
Cont in rib for 4 rows more, ending with a
WS row.
Row 7 (RS): Rib to last 4 sts, yo, P2tog, K2.
Cont in rib for 18 rows more, ending with
a RS row.
Row 26 (WS): Rib 7 and slip these 7 sts onto a
holder, rib to last 0 (0: 1: 1: 0) st, (inc in last st)
0 (0: 1: 1: 0) times. 57 (59: 62: 64: 67) sts.
Change to size 6 (4mm) needles.
Beg with a K row, cont in St st until left front
matches back to beg of armhole shaping,
ending with a WS row.
Shape armhole
Bind/cast off 5 (5: 6: 6: 7) sts at beg of next row.
52 (54: 56: 58: 60) sts.
Work 1 row.
Dec 1 st at armhole edge of next 5 (7: 7: 9: 9)
rows, then on foll 2 (1: 2: 1: 2) alt rows, then
on every foll 4th row until 43 (44: 45: 46: 47)
sts rem.
Work even/straight until 21 (21: 23: 23: 23)
rows less have been worked than on back to
start of shoulder shaping, ending with a RS row.
Shape neck
Bind/cast off 7 (8: 7: 8: 9) sts at beg of next row.
36 (36: 38: 38: 38) sts.

Dec 1 st at neck edge of next 8 rows, then on
foll 3 (3: 4: 4: 4) alt rows, then on foll 4th row.
24 (24: 25: 25: 25) sts.
Work 2 rows, ending with a WS row.
Shape shoulder
Bind/cast off 8 sts at beg of next and foll alt row.
Work 1 row.
Bind/cast off rem 8 (8: 9: 9: 9) sts.

RIGHT FRONT

Cast on 64 (66: 68: 70: 74) sts using size 5
(3¾mm) needles.
Row 1 (RS): K2, *P1, K1, rep from * to end.
Row 2: *P1, K1, rep from * to end.
These 2 rows form rib.
Cont in rib for 23 rows more, ending with a RS
row.
Row 26 (WS): (Inc in first st) 0 (0: 1: 1: 0)
times, rib to last 7 sts and turn, leaving last
7 sts on a holder.
57 (59: 62: 64: 67) sts.
Complete to match left front, reversing shapings.

SLEEVES (both alike)

Cast on 59 (59: 61: 63: 63) sts using size 5
(3¾mm) needles.
Work in rib as given for back for 26 rows,
ending with a WS row.
Change to size 6 (4mm) needles.
Beg with a K row, work in St st for 2 rows,
ending with a WS row.
Row 29 (RS): K2, M1, K to last 2 sts, M1, K2.
Working all increases as set by last row, cont in
St st, shaping sides by inc 1 st at each end of
every foll 8th row to 65 (73: 75: 75: 85) sts,
then on every foll 10th row until there are
81 (83: 85: 87: 89) sts.
Work even/straight until sleeve measures 19¼
(19½: 19½: 20: 20)in/49 (50: 50: 51: 51)cm,
ending with a WS row.
Shape sleeve cap
Bind/cast off 5 (5: 6: 6: 7) sts at beg of next 2
rows. 71 (73: 73: 75: 75) sts.

Dec 1 st at each end of next 3 rows, then on foll 2 alt rows, then on every foll 4th row until 47 (49: 49: 51: 51) sts rem.

Work 1 row, ending with a WS row.

Dec 1 st at each end of next and foll 0 (1: 1: 2: 2) alt rows, then on foll 5 rows, ending with a WS row. Bind/cast off rem 35 sts.

FINISHING

PRESS as described on page 136.

Shoulder patches (make 4)

Cast on 25 (25: 27: 27: 27) sts using size 3 (3¹/₄mm) needles.

Row 1: K1, *P1, K1, rep from * to end.

Row 2: As row 1.

These 2 rows form seed/moss st.

Work in seed/moss st for 38 rows more.

Bind/cast off 8 (8: 9: 9: 9) sts at beg of next and foll alt row.

Work 1 row. Bind/cast off rem 9 sts.

Lay shoulder patches on RS of back and front, matching shaped bound-off/cast-off edges and positioning patch 2 sts in from armhole edge. Sew in place.

Join both shoulder seams using backstitch, or mattress stitch if preferred, enclosing shoulder patches in seam.

Button band

Slip 7 sts left on right front holder onto size 5 (3³/₄mm) needles and rejoin yarn with WS facing.

Cont in rib as set until button band, when slightly stretched, fits up right front opening edge to neck shaping, ending with a WS row. Bind/cast off in rib.

Mark positions for 7 buttons on this band—first to come level with buttonhole already worked in left front, last to come ¹/₂in/1.5cm below neck shaping and rem 5 buttons evenly spaced between.

Buttonhole band

Slip 7 sts left on left front holder onto size 5 (3³/₄mm) needles and rejoin yarn with RS facing.

Cont in rib as set until buttonhole band, when slightly stretched, fits up left front opening edge to neck shaping, ending with a WS row and with the addition of 6 buttonholes more worked to correspond with positions marked for buttons on right front as foll:

Buttonhole row (RS): P1, K1, P1, yo, P2tog, K2.

When band is complete, bind/cast off in rib. Slip stitch bands in place.

Collar

With RS facing and using size 5 (3³/₄mm) needles, starting and ending halfway across top of bands, pick up and knit 34 (35: 36: 37: 38) sts up right side of neck, 37 (39: 39: 41: 43) sts from back, then 34 (35: 36: 37: 38) sts down left side of neck. 105 (109: 111: 115: 119) sts.

Row 1 (WS of body, RS of collar): K2, *P1, K1, rep from * to last st, K1.

Row 2: K1, *P1, K1, rep from * to end.

These 2 rows form rib.

Cont in rib until collar measures 5¹/₂in/14cm. Bind/cast off in rib.

Elbow patches (make 2)

Cast on 9 sts using size 3 (3¹/₄mm) needles.

Work in seed/moss st as given for shoulder patches for 1 row.

Keeping seed/moss st correct, cast on 3 sts at beg of next 2 rows. 15 sts.

Inc 1 st at beg of next 8 rows. 23 sts.

Work 2 rows.

Inc 1 st at beg of next 2 rows. 25 sts.

Work 24 rows.

Dec 1 st at beg of next 2 rows. 23 sts.

Work 2 rows.

Dec 1 st at beg of next 8 rows. 15 sts.

Bind/cast off 3 sts at beg of next 2 rows.

Bind/cast off rem 9 sts.

Using photograph as a guide, lay elbow patches onto RS of sleeves and sew in place.

See page 136 for finishing instructions, setting in sleeves using the set-in method.

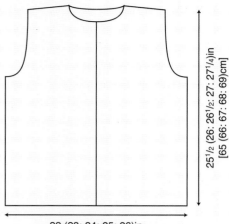

25¹/₂ (26: 26¹/₂: 27: 27¹/₄)in [65 (66: 67: 68: 69)cm]

22 (23: 24: 25: 26)in [56.5 (58.5: 61.5: 63.5: 66.5)cm]

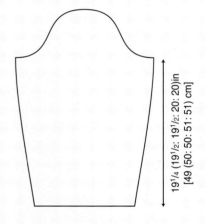

19¹/₄ (19¹/₂: 19¹/₂: 20: 20)in [49 (50: 50: 51: 51) cm]

ORIGAMI
KAFFE FASSETT

This eye-catching sweater encapsulates the rich
colors of the multi-layered autumn woodland
with its carpet of fallen leaves. The inspiration
comes from the artists working in the first half of
the twentieth century—Paul Klee, Robert
Delaunay, and Pablo Picasso.

ORIGAMI
KAFFE FASSETT

YARN AND SIZES

	S	M	L	XL	XXL	
To fit chest	38	40	42	44	46	in
	97	102	107	112	117	cm

Rowan Yorkshire Tweed 4 ply

A = dark purple (no. 280) or desired color

| | 3 | 3 | 3 | 3 | 3 | x 25g |

B = blue-green (no. 271) or desired color

| | 2 | 2 | 3 | 3 | 3 | x 25g |

C = dark rust (no. 278) or desired color

| | 2 | 2 | 2 | 3 | 3 | x 25g |

D = red (no. 275) or desired color

| | 3 | 3 | 4 | 4 | 4 | x 25g |

E = medium purple (no. 276) or desired color

| | 2 | 2 | 2 | 2 | 3 | x 25g |

F = black (no. 283) or desired color

| | 3 | 3 | 3 | 3 | 3 | x 25g |

G = rose (no. 269) or desired color

| | 2 | 2 | 2 | 2 | 2 | x 25g |

H = medium blue (no. 285) or desired color

| | 2 | 2 | 2 | 2 | 2 | x 25g |

J = dark blue-green (no. 282) or desired color

| | 3 | 3 | 3 | 3 | 3 | x 25g |

K = gray-blue (no. 267) or desired color

| | 1 | 1 | 1 | 1 | 2 | x 25g |

L = medium gray (no. 266) or desired color

| | 2 | 2 | 2 | 2 | 2 | x 25g |

M = gray-lilac (no. 268) or desired color

| | 1 | 1 | 1 | 1 | 1 | x 25g |

N = medium rust (no. 273) or desired color

| | 2 | 2 | 2 | 2 | 2 | x 25g |

P = light brown (no. 265) or desired color

| | 1 | 1 | 1 | 1 | 1 | x 25g |

R = medium green (no. 286) or desired color

| | 2 | 2 | 2 | 2 | 2 | x 25g |

S = dark red (no. 279) or desired color

| | 2 | 2 | 2 | 2 | 2 | x 25g |

T = dark brown (no. 284) or desired color

| | 2 | 2 | 2 | 2 | 2 | x 25g |

V = dark blue (no. 281) or desired color

| | 2 | 2 | 2 | 2 | 2 | x 25g |

NEEDLES

1 pair size 2 (2¾mm) needles

1 pair size 3 (3¼mm) needles

GAUGE/TENSION

26 sts and 38 rows to 4in/10cm measured over patterned St st using size 3 (3¼mm) needles.

BACK

Cast on 147 (153: 159: 165: 171) sts using size 2 (2¾mm) needles and yarn A.

**Row 1 (RS): K1, *P1, K1, rep from * to end.

Row 2: P1, *K1, P1, rep from * to end.

These 2 rows form rib.

Joining in and breaking off colors as required, cont in rib in stripes as foll:

Using yarn B, work 2 rows.

Using yarn C, work 2 rows.

Using yarn D, work 2 rows.

Using yarn E, work 2 rows.

Using yarn A, work 2 rows.

Using yarn E, work 2 rows.

Using yarn D, work 2 rows.

Using yarn C, work 2 rows.

Using yarn B, work 2 rows.

Using yarn F, work 2 rows.**

Change to size 3 (3¼mm) needles.

Starting and ending rows as indicated and using the **intarsia** technique (see page 136), cont in patt from chart, which is worked entirely in St st beg with a K row, as foll:

Work even/straight until chart row 114 (114: 118: 118: 122) has been completed, ending with a WS row.

Back should measure 13½ (13¾: 14¼: 14¼: 14¾)in/35 (35: 36: 36: 37)cm.

Shape armholes

Keeping patt correct, bind/cast off 8 sts at beg of next 2 rows.

131 (137: 143: 149: 155) sts.

Dec 1 st at each end of next 5 rows.

121 (127: 133: 139: 145) sts.

Work even/straight until chart row 208 (212: 216: 220: 224) has been completed, ending with a WS row.

Armhole should measure 10 (10¼: 10¼: 10½: 10½)in/25 (26: 26: 27: 27)cm.

Shape shoulders and back neck

Bind/cast off 12 (13: 14: 14: 15) sts at beg of next 2 rows.

97 (101: 105: 111: 115) sts.

Next row (RS): Bind/cast off 12 (13: 14: 14: 15) sts, patt until there are 16 (16: 17: 19: 19) sts on right needle and turn, leaving rem sts on a holder.

Work each side of neck separately.

Bind/cast off 4 sts at beg of next row.

Bind/cast off rem 12 (12: 13: 15: 15) sts.

With RS facing, rejoin yarns to rem sts, bind/cast off center 41 (43: 43: 45: 47) sts, patt to end.

Complete to match first side, reversing shapings.

FRONT

Work as given for back until chart row 186 (190: 192: 196: 200) has been completed, ending with a WS row.

Shape neck

Next row (RS): Patt 51 (53: 57: 59: 61) sts and turn, leaving rem sts on a holder.

Work each side of neck separately.

Bind/cast off 4 sts at beg of next row.

47 (49: 53: 55: 57) sts.

Dec 1 st at neck edge of next 7 rows, then on foll 3 (3: 4: 4: 4) alt rows, then on foll 4th row.

36 (38: 41: 43: 45) sts.

Work 3 rows, ending with a WS row.

Shape shoulder

Bind/cast off 12 (13: 14: 14: 15) sts at beg of next and foll alt row.

Work 1 row.

Bind/cast off rem 12 (12: 13: 15: 15) sts.

With RS facing, rejoin yarns to rem sts, bind/cast off center 19 (21: 19: 21: 23) sts, patt to end.

Complete to match first side, reversing shapings.

SLEEVES (both alike)

Cast on 73 (73: 75: 77: 77) sts using size 2 (2³/4mm) needles and yarn A.

Work as given for back from ** to **.

Change to size 3 (3¹/4mm) needles.

Starting and ending rows as indicated, cont in patt from chart, shaping sides by inc 1 st at each end of 7th and every foll 6th row to 103 (95: 101: 103: 103) sts, then on every foll 4th row until there are 131 (137: 137: 141: 141) sts, taking inc sts into patt.

Work even/straight until chart row 164 (168: 168: 172: 172) has been completed, ending with a WS row. Sleeve should measure 19¹/4 (19¹/2: 19¹/2: 20: 20)in/48 (49: 49: 50: 50)cm.

Shape top of sleeve

Keeping patt correct, bind/cast off 8 sts at beg of next 2 rows.

115 (121: 121: 125: 125) sts.

Dec 1 st at each end of next and foll 5 alt rows.

Work 1 row, ending with a WS row.

Bind/cast off rem 103 (109: 109: 113: 113) sts.

FINISHING

PRESS as described on page 136.

Join right shoulder seam using backstitch, or mattress stitch if preferred.

Neckband

With RS facing, using size 2 (2³/4mm) needles and yarn E, pick up and knit 26 (26: 28: 28: 28) sts down left side of neck, 19 (21: 19: 21: 23) sts from front, 26 (26: 28: 28: 28) sts up right side of neck, then 50 (52: 52: 54: 56) sts from back.

121 (125: 127: 131: 135) sts.

Beg with row 2, work in rib as given for back as foll:

Using yarn E, work 1 row.

Using yarn D, work 2 rows.

Using yarn C, work 2 rows.

Using yarn B, work 2 rows.

Using yarn A, work 1 row.

Using yarn A, bind/cast off in rib (on WS).

See page 136 for finishing instructions, setting in sleeves using the set-in method.

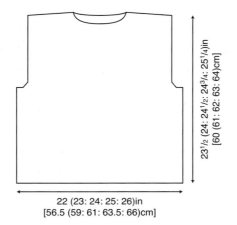

22 (23: 24: 25: 26)in
[56.5 (59: 61: 63.5: 66)cm]

23¹/2 (24: 24¹/2: 24³/4: 25¹/4)in
[60 (61: 62: 63: 64)cm]

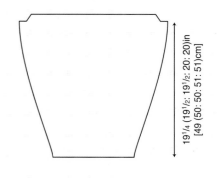

19¹/4 (19¹/2: 19¹/2: 20: 20)in
[49 (50: 50: 51: 51)cm]

ORIGAMI
KAFFE FASSETT

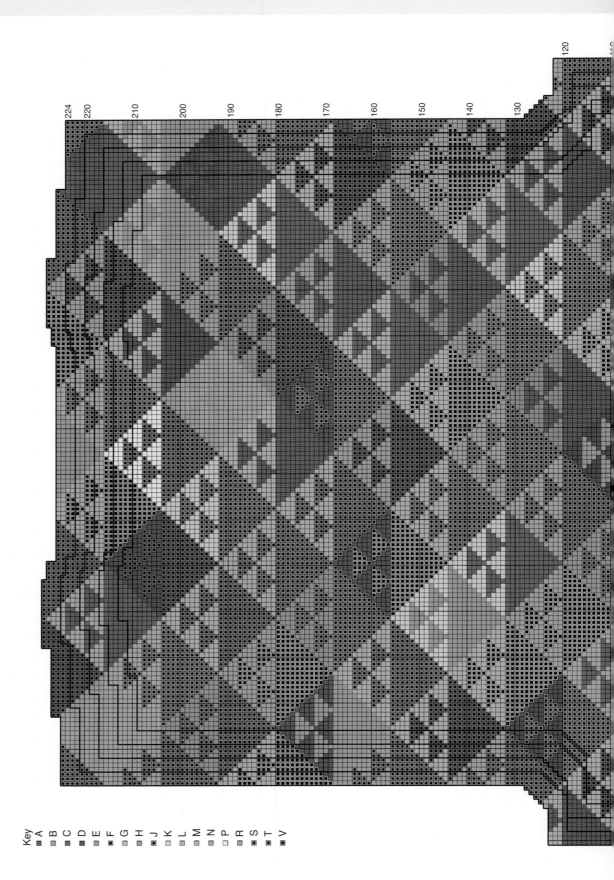

Key A B C D E F G H J K L M N P R S T V

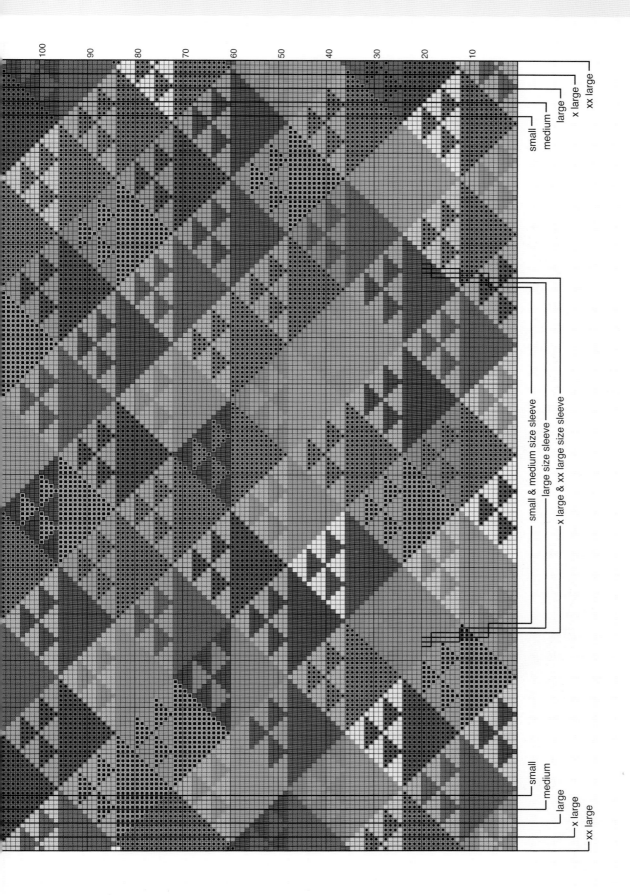

100 90 80 70 60 50 40 30 20 10

small
medium
large
x large
xx large

small & medium size sleeve
large size sleeve
x large & xx large size sleeve

small
medium
large
x large
xx large

MILI
LUCINDA GUY

This little top has a film-star look, remniscent of Audrey Hepburn in the movie *Breakfast at Tiffany's*. The scalloped neck, little sleeves, and wavy edgings give it a real period feel. Any accessories would detract from this jeweled look: it needs no embellishment.

YARN AND SIZES

	XS	S	M	L	XL	
To fit bust	32	34	36	38	40	in
	81	86	91	97	102	cm

Rowan 4 ply Soft

A = pink (no. 377) or desired MC

	5	5	6	6	7	x 50g

B = red (no. 374) or desired 1st CC

	1	1	1	1	1	x 50g

C = burgundy (no. 382) or desired 2nd CC

	1	1	1	1	1	x 50g

D = light turquoise (no. 373) or desired 3rd CC

	1	1	1	1	1	x 50g

E = black (no. 383) or desired 4th CC

	1	1	1	1	1	x 50g

NEEDLES AND CROCHET HOOK

1 pair size 2 (2³/₄mm) needles
1 pair size 3 (3¹/₄mm) needles
Size B-1 (2.00mm) crochet hook

GAUGE/TENSION

28 sts and 36 rows to 4in/10cm measured over St st using size 3 (3¹/₄mm) needles.

CROCHET ABBREVIATIONS

sc = single crochet (double crochet in UK)
ch = chain.

BACK

Cast on 114 (121: 129: 136: 142) sts using size 2 (2³/₄mm) needles and yarn E.
Row 1 (RS): K6 (1: 5: 0: 3), *K1, P2, K2tog tbl, (K1, yo) 6 times, K1, K2tog, P2, K1, rep from * to last 6 (1: 5: 0: 3) sts, K6 (1: 5: 0: 3).
138 (149: 157: 168: 174) sts.
Row 2: P6 (1: 5: 0: 3), *P1, K2, P15, K2, P1, rep from * to last 6 (1: 5: 0: 3) sts, P6 (1: 5: 0: 3).

Row 3: K6 (1: 5: 0: 3), *K1, P2, K3tog tbl, K9, K3tog, P2, K1, rep from * to last 6 (1: 5: 0: 3) sts, K6 (1: 5: 0: 3).
114 (121: 129: 136: 142) sts.
Row 4: P6 (1: 5: 0: 3), *P1, K2, P11, K2, P1, rep from * to last 6 (1: 5: 0: 3) sts, P6 (1: 5: 0: 3).
These 4 rows form patt.
Joining in and breaking off colors as required, cont in patt in stripes as foll:
Using yarn C, work 4 rows.
Using yarn B, work 4 rows.
Using yarn A, work 4 rows.
Using yarn C, work 4 rows.
Using yarn B, work 4 rows.
Using yarn A, work 4 rows.
Using yarn B, work 4 rows.
Using yarn A, work 4 rows, inc (-: -: dec: inc) 1 (-: -: 1: 1) st at end of last row.
115 (121: 129: 135: 143) sts.
Break off contrasting yarns and cont using yarn A only.
Change to size 3 (3¹/₄mm) needles.
Beg with a K row, work in St st for 2 rows, ending with a WS row.
Starting and ending rows as indicated and using the **intarsia** technique (see page 136), work in patt from chart for border for 8 rows, ending with a WS row.
Break off contrasting yarns and cont in St st using yarn A only.
Inc 1 st at each end of 11th and foll 20th row.
119 (125: 133: 139: 147) sts.
Work even/straight until back measures 12 (12¹/₂: 12³/₄: 13¹/₄: 13¹/₄)in/27 (28: 28: 29: 29)cm, ending with a WS row.

Shape armholes

Bind/cast off 4 (5: 5: 6: 6) sts at beg of next 2

rows, then 3 sts at beg of foll 2 rows.
105 (109: 117: 121: 129) sts.
Dec 1 st at each end of next 5 (5: 7: 7: 9) rows, then on foll 1 (2: 2: 3: 3) alt rows, then on foll 4th row.
91 (93: 97: 99: 103) sts.
Work even/straight until armhole measures 6 (6: 6¹/₄: 6¹/₄: 6³/₄)in/15 (15: 16: 16: 17)cm, ending with a WS row.
Starting and ending rows as indicated and using the **intarsia** technique, work in patt from chart for back neck for 12 rows, ending with a WS row.
Break off contrasting yarns and cont in St st using yarn A only.
Work 2 rows, ending with a WS row.

Shape shoulders and back neck

Bind/cast off 7 (7: 8: 8: 8) sts at beg of next 2 rows. 77 (79: 81: 83: 87) sts.
Next row (RS): Bind/cast off 7 (7: 8: 8: 8) sts, K until there are 11 (11: 11: 11: 13) sts on right needle and turn, leaving rem sts on a holder.
Work each side of neck separately.
Bind/cast off 4 sts at beg of next row.
Bind/cast off rem 7 (7: 7: 7: 9) sts.
With RS facing, rejoin yarn to rem sts, bind/cast off center 41 (43: 43: 45: 45) sts, K to end.
Complete to match first side, reversing shapings.

FRONT

Work as given for back until 4 rows less have been worked than on back to beg of armhole shaping, ending with a WS row.
Next row (RS): Using yarn A, K48 (51: 55: 58: 62); work next 23 sts as row 1 of chart for motif; using yarn A, K to end.
Next row: Using yarn A, P48 (51: 55: 58: 62); work next 23 sts as row 2 of chart for motif;

MILI

LUCINDA GUY

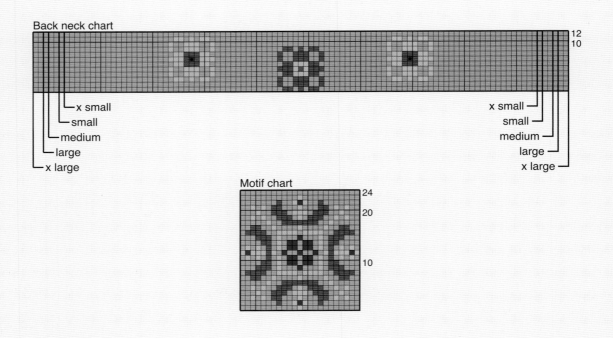

Back neck chart

12
10

x small
small
medium
large
x large

x small
small
medium
large
x large

Motif chart

24
20

10

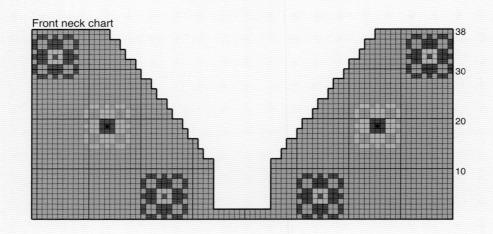

Front neck chart

38
30

20

10

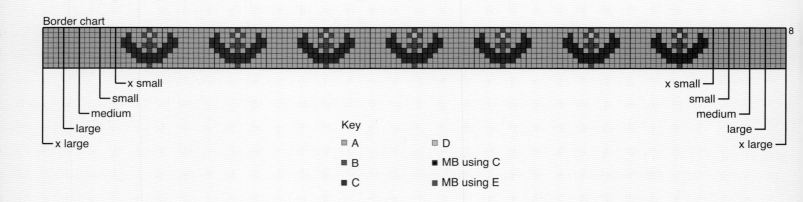

Border chart

8

x small
small
medium
large
x large

x small
small
medium
large
x large

Key

■ A   ☐ D

■ B   ■ MB using C

■ C   ■ MB using E

using yarn A, P to end.

These 2 rows set the sts—center 23 sts foll chart for motif and rem sts in St st using yarn A.

Working rem 22 rows of chart for motif and then working sts above chart in St st using yarn A, cont as foll:

Work 2 rows, ending with a WS row.

Shape armholes

Keeping chart correct, bind/cast off 4 (5: 5: 6: 6) sts at beg of next 2 rows, then 3 sts at beg of foll 2 rows.

105 (109: 117: 121: 129) sts.

Dec 1 st at each end of next 5 (5: 7: 7: 9) rows, then on foll 1 (2: 2: 3: 3) alt rows, then on foll 4th row.

91 (93: 97: 99: 103) sts.

Work even/straight until 42 (42: 42: 44: 44) rows less have been worked than on back to start of shoulder shaping, ending with a WS row.

Next row (RS): Using yarn A, K5 (6: 8: 9: 11); work next 81 sts as row 1 of chart for front neck; using yarn A, K to end.

Next row: Using yarn A, P5 (6: 8: 9: 11); work next 81 sts as row 2 of chart for front neck; using yarn A, P to end.

These 2 rows set the sts—center 81 sts foll chart for front neck and rem sts in St st using yarn A.

Working rem 36 rows of chart for front neck and then working sts above chart in St st using yarn A, cont as foll:

Divide for neck

Next row (RS): Patt 40 (41: 43: 44: 46) sts and turn, leaving rem sts on a holder.

Work each side of neck separately.

Work 9 rows, ending with a WS row.

Next row (RS): Patt to last 5 sts, K3tog tbl, K2.

Work 1 row.

Next row: Patt to last 4 sts, K2tog tbl, K2.

Work 1 row.

Rep last 4 rows 5 (5: 5: 6: 6) times more.

22 (23: 25: 23: 25) sts.

Next row (RS): Patt to last 4 (5: 5: 0: 0) sts, (K2tog tbl, K2) 1 (0: 0: 0: 0) times, (K3tog tbl,

K2) 0 (1: 1: 0: 0) times. 21 (21: 23: 23: 25) sts.

Work 5 (5: 5: 3: 3) rows, ending with a WS row.

Shape shoulder

Bind/cast off 7 (7: 8: 8: 8) sts at beg of next and foll alt row.

Work 1 row.

Bind/cast off rem 7 (7: 7: 7: 9) sts.

With RS facing, rejoin yarn to rem sts, bind/cast off center 11 sts, patt to end.

Work 9 rows, ending with a WS row.

Next row (RS): K2, K3tog, patt to end.

Work 1 row.

Next row: K2, K2tog, patt to end.

Work 1 row.

Complete to match first side, reversing shapings.

SLEEVES (both alike)

Cast on 83 (85: 89: 91: 95) sts using size 3 (3¼mm) needles and yarn A.

Beg with a K row, work in St st for 6 rows, ending with a WS row.

Inc 1 st at each end of next and foll 6th row, then on every foll 4th row until there are 91 (93: 97: 99: 103) sts.

Work 9 rows, ending with a WS row.

Shape sleeve cap

Bind/cast off 4 (5: 5: 6: 6) sts at beg of next 2 rows, then 3 sts at beg of foll 2 rows.

77 (77: 81: 81: 85) sts.

Dec 1 st at each end of next 5 rows, then on foll 3 alt rows, then on every foll 4th row until 49 (49: 53: 53: 57) sts rem.

Work 1 row, ending with a WS row.

Dec 1 st at each end of next and every foll alt row to 37 sts, then on foll 3 rows, end with a WS row.

Bind/cast off rem 31 sts.

FINISHING

PRESS as described on page 136.

Join both shoulder seams using backstitch, or mattress stitch if preferred.

Neck edging

With RS facing, using size B-1 (2.00mm) crochet hook and yarn A, rejoin yarn at right shoulder seam and work one round of sc evenly around entire neck edge, working 2sc in corners and ensuring edging lays flat, join with a slip st in first sc, turn.

Breaking off and joining in colors as required, cont as foll:

Next round: Using yarn E, ch1 (does NOT count as st), 1sc in each sc to end, skipping sc and working extra as required to ensure edging lays flat, join with a slip st in first sc, turn.

Using yarn C, rep last round once.

Using yarn B, rep last round once.

Using yarn A, rep last round once.

Fasten off.

See page 136 for finishing instructions, setting in sleeves using the set-in method. Work edging around cast-on edge of sleeves to match neck edging.

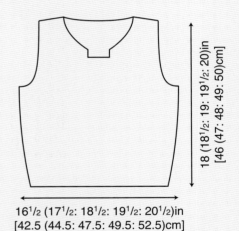

16½ (17½: 18½: 19½: 20½)in
[42.5 (44.5: 47.5: 49.5: 52.5)cm]

18 (18½: 19: 19½: 20)in
[46 (47: 48: 49: 50)cm]

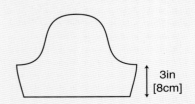

3in
[8cm]

ALOUETTE
SARAH DALLAS

This top has a definite '50s flavor with its wavy lines and elbow length sleeves.
It is feminine and light, making the ideal match for this ballet-style layered skirt,
giving a look that is both fun and glamorous.

YARN AND SIZES

	XS	S	M	L	XL	
To fit bust	32	34	36	38	40	in
	81	86	91	97	102	cm

Rowan 4 ply Soft

A = light brown (no. 386) or desired MC

| | 3 | 3 | 4 | 4 | 4 | x 50g |

B = dusty rose (no. 378) or desired 1st CC

| | 2 | 2 | 3 | 3 | 3 | x 50g |

C = dark brown (no. 389) or desired 2nd CC

| | 1 | 1 | 1 | 1 | 1 | x 50g |

D = burgundy (no. 382) or desired 3rd CC

| | 1 | 1 | 1 | 1 | 2 | x 50g |

NEEDLES

1 pair size 2 (2¾mm) needles
1 pair size 3 (3¼mm) needles

GAUGE/TENSION

30 sts and 34 rows to 4in/10cm measured over
pattern using size 3 (3¼mm) needles.

PATTERN NOTE

In order to ensure pattern is kept correct, place a
marker on needle at beg of first full patt rep and
at end of last full patt rep. When working sts on
each side of these markers, ensure a decrease is
made for every increase so that number of sts
remain correct.

BACK

Cast on 111 (117: 125: 131: 137) sts using
size 2 (2¾mm) needles and yarn D.
Break off yarn D and join in yarn A.
Row 1 (RS): K1, *P1, K1, rep from * to end.
Row 2: P1, *K1, P1, rep from * to end.
These 2 rows form rib.
Work in rib for 2¼in/6cm, ending with a RS row.

Next row (WS): Rib 3 (2: 6: 5: 4), M1,
*rib 4, M1, rep from * to last 4 (3: 7: 6: 5) sts,
rib to end.
138 (146: 154: 162: 170) sts.
Change to size 3 (3¼mm) needles.
Row 1 (RS): Knit.
Row 2: K3 (0: 0: 0: 1), P6 (0: 0: 3: 6), K6 (1:
5: 6: 6), *K6, P6, K6, rep from * to last 15 (1:
5: 9: 13) sts, K6 (1: 5: 6: 6), P6 (0: 0: 3: 6),
K3 (0: 0: 0: 1).
Row 3: K3 (1: 2: 3: 1), (K2tog) 1 (0: 0: 0: 1)
times, (K1, yo) 4 (0: 1: 2: 4) times, (K2tog) 3
(0: 1: 2: 3) times, *(K2tog) 3 times, (K1, yo) 6
times, (K2tog) 3 times, rep from * to last 15 (1:
5: 9: 13) sts, (K2tog) 3 (0: 1: 2: 3) times, (K1,
yo) 4 (0: 1: 2: 4) times, (K2tog) 1 (0: 0: 0: 1)
times, K3 (1: 2: 3: 1).
Row 4: Purl.
These 4 rows form patt.
Keeping patt correct and using yarns A, B, C,
and D, cont in stripes as foll:
Using yarn C, work 2 rows.
Using yarn A, work 2 rows.
Using yarn C, work 2 rows.
Using yarn A, work 6 rows.
Using yarn B, work 8 rows.
Using yarn D, work 2 rows.
Using yarn A, work 2 rows.
Using yarn D, work 2 rows.
Using yarn B, work 8 rows.
Using yarn A, work 2 rows.
Last 40 rows form stripe sequence.
Cont in patt and stripes until back measures
11½ (11¾: 11¾: 12: 12¼)in/28 (29: 29: 30:
30)cm, ending with a WS row.

Shape armholes

Keeping patt correct, bind/cast off 5 (6: 6: 7: 7)
sts at beg of next 2 rows, then 4 sts at beg of

foll 2 rows.
120 (126: 134: 140: 148) sts.
Dec 1 st at each end of next 5 (5: 7: 7: 9) rows,
then on foll 1 (2: 2: 3: 3) alt rows, then on foll
4th row. 106 (110: 114: 118: 122) sts.
Work even/straight until armhole measures 7½
(7½: 8: 8: 8¼)in/19 (19: 20: 20: 21)cm, ending
with a WS row.

Shape back neck

Next row (RS): Patt 28 (29: 31: 32: 34) sts and
turn, leaving rem sts on a holder.
Work each side of neck separately.
Work 3 rows, ending with a WS row.

Shape shoulder

Bind/cast off 9 (10: 10: 11: 11) sts at beg of
next and foll alt row.
Work 1 row. Bind/cast off rem 10 (9: 11: 10:
12) sts.
With RS facing, rejoin appropriate yarn to
rem sts, bind/cast off center 50 (52: 52: 54: 54)
sts, patt to end.
Complete to match first side, reversing shaping.

FRONT

Work as given for back until 24 rows less have
been worked than on back to start of shoulder
shaping, ending with a WS row.

Shape front neck

Next row (RS): Patt 28 (29: 31: 32: 34) sts and
turn, leaving rem sts on a holder.
Work each side of neck separately.
Work 23 rows, ending with a WS row.

Shape shoulder

Bind/cast off 9 (10: 10: 11: 11) sts at beg of
next and foll alt row.
Work 1 row. Bind/cast off rem 10 (9: 11: 10:
12) sts.
With RS facing, rejoin appropriate yarn to

rem sts, bind/cast off center 50 (52: 52: 54: 54) sts, patt to end.

Complete to match first side, reversing shaping.

SLEEVES (both alike)

Cast on 81 (81: 83: 85: 85) sts using size 2 (2³/4mm) needles and yarn D.

Break off yarn D and join in yarn A.

Work in rib as given for back for 1¹/4in/3cm, ending with a RS row.

Next row (WS): Rib 4 (5: 5: 6: 2), M1, *rib 9 (7: 6: 6: 5), M1, rep from * to last 5 (6: 6: 7: 3) sts, rib to end. 90 (92: 96: 98: 102) sts.

Change to size 3 (3¹/4mm) needles. Join in B.

Row 1 (RS): Knit.

Row 2: K0 (1: 3: 4: 6), *K6, P6, K6, rep from * to last 0 (1: 3: 4: 6) sts, K0 (1: 3: 4: 6).

Row 3: K0 (1: 3: 2: 4), (yo, K2tog) 0 (0: 0: 1: 1) times, *(K2tog) 3 times, (K1, yo) 6 times, (K2tog) 3 times, rep from * to last 0 (1: 3: 4: 6) sts, (K2tog, yo) 0 (0: 0: 1: 1) times, K0 (1: 3: 2: 4).

Row 4: Purl.

These 4 rows form patt.

Working 4 rows more using yarn B (and then 2 rows using yarn D), cont in patt and stripe sequence as given for back until sleeve measures 4¹/4in/11cm, ending with a WS row.

Shape sleeve cap

Keeping patt and stripes correct, bind/cast off 5 (6: 6: 7: 7) sts at beg of next 2 rows, then 4 sts at beg of foll 2 rows. 72 (72: 76: 76: 80) sts.

Dec 1 st at each end of next 5 rows, then on foll 2 alt rows, then on every foll 4th row until 48 (48: 52: 52: 56) sts rem.

Work 1 row, ending with a WS row.

Dec 1 st at each end of next and every foll alt row to 40 sts, then on foll 5 rows, ending with a WS row. 30 sts.

Bind/cast off 6 sts at beg of next 2 rows.

Bind/cast off rem 18 sts.

FINISHING

PRESS as described on page 136.

Join right shoulder seam using backstitch, or mattress stitch if preferred.

Neckband

With RS facing, using size 2 (2³/4mm) needles and yarn A, pick up and knit 22 (22: 22: 24: 24) sts down left side of front neck, 1 st from corner (mark this st), 49 (51: 51: 53: 53) sts from front, 1 st from corner (mark this st), 22 (22: 22: 24: 24) sts up right side of front neck, 7 sts down right side of back neck, 1 st from corner (mark this st), 49 (51: 51: 53: 53) sts from back, 1 st from corner (mark this st), then 7 sts up left side of back neck.
160 (164: 164: 172: 172) sts.

Row 1 (WS): *K1, P1, rep from * to end.

This row sets position of rib.

Keeping rib correct, cont as foll:

Row 2: *Rib to within 2 sts of marked st, P2tog, K marked st, P2tog tbl, rep from * 3 times more, rib to end.

Row 3: *Rib to marked st, P marked st, rep from * 3 times more, rib to end.

Rep last 2 rows twice more.

Bind/cast off in rib, still decreasing on each side of marked sts as before.

See page 136 for finishing instructions, setting in sleeves using the set-in method.

19 (19¹/4: 19³/4: 20: 20¹/2)in
[48 (49: 50: 51: 52)cm]

18 (19: 20¹/4: 21¹/4: 22¹/4)in
[46 (48.5: 51.5: 54: 56.5)cm]

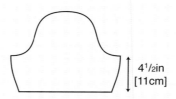

4¹/2in
[11cm]

BUYING YARNS

Rowan yarns (and buttons and beads) have been used for all the knitting patterns in this book. See page 137 for descriptions of the yarns used. To find out where to buy Rowan yarns near you, contact one of the Rowan yarn distributors given below. The main Rowan office is in the United Kingdom (see below for their website).

ROWAN YARN DISTRIBUTORS

U.S.A.
Westminster Fibers Inc,
165 Ledge Street, Nashua, New Hampshire 03060
Tel: 1-800-445-9276
www.westminsterfibers.com

U.K.
Rowan, Green Lane Mill, Holmfirth,
West Yorkshire, HD9 2DX
Tel: +44 (0) 1484 681881
Fax: +44 (0) 1484 687920
Email: mail@knitrowan.com
www.knitrowan.com

AUSTRALIA
Australian Country Spinners, Pty Ltd,
Level 7, 409 St. Kilda Road, Melbourne Vic 3004
Tel: 03 9380 3830
Fax: 03 9820 0989
Email: sales@auspinners.com.au

AUSTRIA
Coats Harlander GmbH, Autokaderstrasse 31,
A-1210 Wien.
Tel: (01) 27716 - 0
Fax: (01) 27716 - 228

BELGIUM
Coats Benelux, Ring Oost 14A, Ninove, 9400,
Belgium
Tel: 0346 35 37 00
Email: sales.coatsninove@coats.com

CANADA
Westminster Fibers Inc,
165 Ledge Street, Nashua, New Hampshire 03060
Tel: 1-800-445-9276
www.westminsterfibers.com

CHINA
Coats Shanghai Ltd, No 9 Building, Baosheng Road,
Songjiang Industrial Zone, Shanghai.
Tel: (86-21) 5774 3733
Fax: (86-21) 5774 3768

DENMARK
Coats Danmark A/S, Nannasgade 28,
2200 Kobenhavn N
Tel: (45) 35 86 90 50
Fax: (45) 35 82 15 10
Email: info@hpgruppen.dk
www.hpgruppen.dk

FINLAND
Coats Opti Oy, Ketjutie 3, 04220 Kerava
Tel: (358) 9 274 871
Fax: (358) 9 2748 7330
Email: coatsopti.sales@coats.com

FRANCE
Coats France / Steiner Frères,
SAS 100, avenue du Général de Gaulle,
18 500 Mehun-Sur-Yèvre
Tel: (33) 02 48 23 12 30
Fax: (33) 02 48 23 12 40

GERMANY
Coats GmbH, Kaiserstrasse 1, D-79341 Kenzingen
Tel: (49) 7644 8020
Fax: (49) 7644 802399
www.coatsgmbh.de

HOLLAND
Coats Benelux, Ring Oost 14A, Ninove, 9400,
Belgium
Tel: 0346 35 37 00
Email: sales.coatsninove@coats.com

HONG KONG
Coats China Holdings Ltd, 19/F Millennium City 2,
378 Kwun Tong Road, Kwun Tong, Kowloon
Tel: (852) 2798 6886
Fax: (852) 2305 0311

ICELAND
Storkurinn, Laugavegi 59, 101 Reykjavik
Tel: (354) 551 8258
Email: storkurinn@simnet.is

ITALY
Coats Cucirini s.r.l., Via Sarca 223, 20126 Milano
Tel: 800 992377
Fax: 0266111701
Email: servizio.clienti@coats.com

KOREA
Coats Korea Co Ltd, 5F Kuckdong B/D,
935-40 Bangbae- Dong, Seocho-Gu, Seoul
Tel: (82) 2 521 6262.
Fax: (82) 2 521 5181

LEBANON
y.knot, Saifi Village, Mkhalissiya Street 162, Beirut
Tel: (961) 1 992211
Fax: (961) 1 315553
Email: y.knot@cyberia.net.lb

LUXEMBOURG
Coats Benelux, Ring Oost 14A, Ninove, 9400,
Belgium
Tel: 054 318989
Email: sales.coatsninove@coats.com

MALTA
John Gregory Ltd, 8 Ta'Xbiex Sea Front,
Msida MSD 1512.
Tel: (356) 2133 0202
Fax: (356) 2134 4745,
Email: raygreg@onvol.net

MEXICO
Estambres Crochet SA de CV, Aaron Saenz
1891-7, Monterrey, NL 64650.
Tel: +52 (81) 8335-3870

NEW ZEALAND
ACS New Zealand, 1 March Place, Belfast,
Christchurch
Tel: 64-3-323-6665
Fax: 64-3-323-6660

NORWAY
Coats Knappehuset AS, Pb 100 Ulset, 5873 Bergen
Tel: (47) 55 53 93 00
Fax: (47) 55 53 93 93

SINGAPORE
Golden Dragon Store,
101 Upper Cross Street #02-51, People's Park Centre,
Singapore 058357
Tel: (65) 6 5358454
Fax: (65) 6 2216278
Email: gdscraft@hotmail.com

SOUTH AFRICA
Arthur Bales LTD, 62 4th Avenue, Linden 2195
Tel: (27) 11 888 2401
Fax: (27) 11 782 6137
Email: arthurb@new.co.za

SPAIN
Coats Fabra, Santa Adria 20, 08030 Barcelona
Tel: 932908400
Fax: 932908409
Email: atencion.clientes@coats.com

SWEDEN
Coats Expotex AB, Division Craft,
Box 297, 401 24 Goteborg
Tel: (46) 33 720 79 00
Fax: (46) 31 47 16 50

SWITZERLAND
Coats Stroppel AG, Stroppelstr.16
CH -5300 Turgi (AG)
Tel: (41) 562981220
Fax: (41) 56 298 12 50

TAIWAN
Cactus Quality Co Ltd, P.O.Box 30 485, Taipei,
Taiwan, R.O.C., Office: 7FL-2, No 140, Roosevelt
Road, Sec 2,Taipei, Taiwan, R.O.C.
Tel: 886-2-23656527
Fax: 886-2-23656503
Email: cqcl@m17.hinet.net

THAILAND
Global Wide Trading, 10 Lad Prao Soi 88,
Bangkok 10310
Tel: 00 662 933 9019
Fax: 00 662 933 9110
Email: global.wide@yahoo.com

GAUGE/TENSION

Obtaining the correct gauge/tension can make the difference between a successful garment and a disastrous one. It controls both the shape and size of an article, so any variation, however slight, can distort the finished garment.

Different designers feature in this book and it is **their** gauge/tension, given at the **start** of each pattern, that you must match. To check your gauge/tension, knit a square in the pattern stitch and/or stockinette/stocking stitch of perhaps 5–10 more stitches and 5–10 more rows than those given in the gauge/tension note. Press the finished square under a damp cloth and mark out the central 4in/10cm square with pins. If you have too many stitches to 4in/10cm, try again using thicker needles. If you have too few stitches to 4in/10cm, try again using finer needles. Once you have achieved the correct gauge/tension, your garment will be knitted to the measurements shown in the size diagram with the pattern.

SIZING AND SIZE DIAGRAM NOTE

The instructions are given for the smallest size, and larger sizes follow in parentheses. If there is only **one set of figures,** it refers to all sizes. If - (hyphen) or 0 (zero) is given in an instruction for the size you are knitting, then that particular instruction does not apply to your size.

Included with every pattern in this book is a **size diagram** of the finished garment pieces and their dimensions. The size diagram shows the finished width of the garment at the underarm point, and it is this measurement that you should choose first; a useful tip is to measure one of your own garments that is a comfortable fit. Having chosen a size based on width, look at the corresponding length for that size; if you are not happy with the total recommended length, adjust your own garment before beginning your armhole shaping—any adjustment after this point will mean that your sleeve will not fit into your garment easily. Don't forget to take your adjustment into account if there is any side-seam shaping.

Finally, look at the sleeve length; the size diagram shows the finished sleeve measurement, taking into account any top-arm insertion length. Measure your body between the center of your neck and your wrist, this measurement should correspond to half the garment width plus the sleeve length. Again, your sleeve length may be adjusted, but remember to take into consideration your sleeve increases if you do adjust the length—you must increase more frequently than the pattern states to shorten your sleeve, less frequently to lengthen it.

CHART NOTE

Many of the patterns in the book are worked from charts. Each square on a chart represents a stitch and each line of squares a row of knitting. Each color used is given a different symbol or letter and these are shown near the beginning of the pattern, or in the **key** alongside the chart of each pattern. When working from the charts, read odd rows (knit) from right to left and even rows (purl) from left to right, unless otherwise stated.

COLORWORK KNITTING

There are two main methods of working color into a knitted fabric— the **intarsia** and **Fair Isle** techniques. The first method produces a single thickness of fabric and is usually used where a color is only required in a particular area of a row and does not form a repeating pattern across the row, as in the Fair Isle technique.

Intarsia: Cut short lengths of yarn for each motif or block of color used in a row. Then joining in the various colors at the appropriate point on the row, link one color to the next by twisting them around each other where they meet on the wrong side to avoid gaps. All ends can either be darned along the color join lines, as each motif is completed or then can be knitted into the fabric of the knitting as each color is worked into the pattern. This is done in much the same way as "weaving in" yarns when working the Fair Isle technique and does save time darning in ends. It is essential that the gauge/tension is noted for **intarsia** as this may vary from the stockinette/stocking stitch if both are used in the same pattern.

Fair Isle color knitting: When two or three colors are worked repeatedly across a row, strand the yarn **not** in use loosely behind the stitches being worked. If you are working with more than two colors, treat the floating yarns as if they were one yarn and always spread the stitches to their correct width to keep them elastic. It is advisable not to carry the stranded or floating yarns over more than three stitches at a time, but to weave them under and over the color you are working. The floating yarns are therefore caught into the back (wrong side) of the work.

KNITTING RIBBING

ALL ribbing should be knitted firmly; for some knitters, it may be necessary to use a smaller needle size. In order to prevent sagging cuffs, you can use a "knitting-in" elastic.

CROCHET TERMS

US crochet terms and abbreviations have been used throughout. The list below gives the UK equivalent where they vary.

Abbreviation	US	UK
sc	single crochet	double crochet (dc)
hdc	half double	half treble (htr)
dc	double	treble (tr)
tr	treble	double treble (dtr)
dtr	double treble	triple treble (trtr)
trtr	triple treble	quadruple treble (qtr)

SLIP STITCH EDGINGS

When a row-end edge forms the actual finished edge of a garment, you can work a slip stitch edging along this edge for a neat finish.

At the end of a RS row: Work across the row until there is one stitch left on the left needle. Pick up the loop lying between the needles and place this loop on the right needle. Please note that this loop does NOT count as a stitch and is not included in any stitch counts. Now slip the last stitch knitwise with the yarn at the back (wrong side) of the work. At the

beginning of the next row purl together the first (slipped) stitch with the picked-up loop.

At the end of a WS row: Work across the row until there is one stitch left on the left needle. Pick up the loop lying between the needles and place this loop on the right needle. Please note that this loop does NOT count as a stitch and is not included in any stitch counts. Now slip the last stitch purlwise with the yarn at the front (wrong side) of the work. At the beginning of the next row knit together the first (slipped) stitch with the picked-up loop through the back of the loops.

FINISHING INSTRUCTIONS

After working for hours knitting a garment, it is worthwhile finishing them with care. Follow the tips below for a truly professional-looking garment.

PRESSING

Before blocking and pressing, darn in all ends neatly along the selvage edge or a color join, as appropriate. Be sure to **refer to the yarn label for pressing instructions** before ironing.

Block out each piece of knitting using pins and gently press each piece (avoiding the ribbing and garter stitch), using a warm iron over a damp cloth. **Tip**: Take special care to press the edges, as this will make sewing up both easier and neater.

STITCHING PIECES TOGETHER

When stitching the pieces together, remember to match areas of color and texture very carefully where they meet. Use a seam stitch such as backstitch or mattress stitch for all main knitting seams and join all ribbing and neckbands with a flat seam, unless otherwise stated.

Having completed the pattern instructions, join the left shoulder and neckband seams as explained above. Then sew the top of the sleeve to the body of the garment using the method given in the pattern, referring to the appropriate guide below.
Straight bound-off/cast-off sleeves: Place the center of the bound-off/cast-off edge of the sleeve at the shoulder seam. Sew the top of the sleeve to the body, using markers as guidelines where applicable.
Square set-in sleeves: Set the top of the sleeve into the armhole, so that the straight sides at the top of the sleeve form a neat right-angle to the bound-off/cast-off stitches at the armhole on the back and the front.
Shallow set-in sleeves: Join the bound-off/cast-off stitches at the beginning of the armhole shaping to the bound-off/cast-off stitches at the start of the sleeve cap shaping. Sew the sleeve cap into the armhole, easing in the shapings.
Set-in sleeves: Set in the sleeve, easing the sleeve cap into the armhole.

FINAL FINISHING TOUCHES

Join the side and sleeve seams. Slip stitch any pocket edgings and pocket linings into place.

After all the seams are complete, press the seams and hems.

Lastly, sew on the buttons to correspond with the positions of the buttonholes.

SKILL LEVELS

Each of the patterns in this book is marked with a knitting skill level at the beginning of the instructions—easy, average, or experienced. The skill level is indicated by one, two, or three circles (see below). If you are new to knitting or haven't knit for some time, it is best to start with an easy pattern and progress through the next two levels.

⬤ = Easy, straightforward knitting

⬤⬤ = Suitable for the average knitter

⬤⬤⬤ = For the more experienced knitter

ABBREVIATIONS

The knitting pattern abbreviations used in this book are as below.

alt	alternate
approx	approximate
beg	begin(s)(ning)
CC	contrasting color
cm	centimeters
cn	cable needle
cont	continu(e)(ing)
dec	decreas(e)(ing)
foll	follow(s)(ing)
garter st	garter stitch (K every row)
in	inch(es)
inc	increas(e)(ing)
K	knit
m	meter(s)
M1	make one stitch by picking up horizontal loop before next stitch and knitting into back of it
M1P	make one stitch by picking up horizontal loop before next stitch and purling into back of it
MC	main color
mm	millimeters
P	purl
patt	pattern
psso	pass slipped stitch over
p2sso	pass two slipped stitches over
rem	remain(s)(ing)
rep	repeat
rev St st	reverse stockinette/stocking stitch
RS	right side
skp	sl 1, K1, psso
sl 1	slip one stitch
st(s)	stitch(es)
St st	stockinette/stocking stitch (1 row K, 1 row P)
tbl	through back of loop(s)
tog	together
WS	wrong side
yd	yard(s)
yo	yarn over

YARN DESCRIPTIONS

For the best results, use the yarns recommended in the patterns. The yarns used in this book are Rowan yarns (see page 135 for how to obtain Rowan yarns). If, however, you are attempting to use a substitute yarn, be sure to use a yarn that matches the original in type, and buy according to length of yarn per ball, rather than by the weight of the ball.

The specifications of the yarns used in this book are given below. **Shade numbers** are provided with each knitting pattern, but these are only suggestions. Shades change frequently with fashion trends.

Rowan Felted Tweed
A medium-weight wool-mix yarn; 50 percent merino wool, 25 percent alpaca, 25 percent viscose; approx 191yd/175m per 50g ball; recommended gauge/tension—22–24 sts and 30–32 rows to 4in/10cm using sizes 5–6 (3¾–4mm) needles.

Rowan 4 ply Soft
A lightweight wool yarn; 100 percent merino wool; approx 191yd/175m per 50g ball; recommended gauge/tension—28 sts and 36 rows to 4in/10cm using size 3 (3¼mm) needles.

Rowan Kid Classic
A medium-weight mohair-mix yarn; 70 percent lambswool, 26 percent kid mohair, 4 percent nylon; approx 153yd/140m per 50g ball; recommended gauge/tension—18–19 sts and 23–25 rows to 4in/10cm using sizes 8–9 (5–5½mm) needles.

Rowan Kid Silk Haze
A lightweight mohair-mix yarn; 70 percent super kid mohair, 30 percent silk; approx 229yd/210m per 25g ball; recommended gauge/tension—18–25 sts and 23–34 rows to 4in/10cm using sizes 3–8 (3¼–5mm) needles.

Rowan Yorkshire Tweed Aran
An Aran-weight wool yarn; 100 percent pure new wool; approx 175yd/160m per 100g ball; recommended gauge/tension—16 sts and 23 rows to 4in/10cm using sizes 8–9 (5–5½mm) needles.

Rowan Yorkshire Tweed Chunky
A bulky-weight wool yarn; 100 percent pure new wool; approx 109yd/100m per 100g ball; recommended gauge/tension—12 sts and 16 rows to 4in/10cm using size 11 (8mm) needles.

Rowan Yorkshire Tweed DK
A medium-weight wool yarn; 100 percent pure new wool; approx 123yd/113m per 50g ball; recommended gauge/tension—20–22 sts and 28–30 rows to 4in/10cm using size 6 (4mm) needles.

Rowan Yorkshire Tweed 4 ply
A lightweight wool yarn; 100 percent pure new wool; approx 120yd/110m per 25g ball; recommended gauge/tension—26–28 sts and 38–40 rows to 4in/10cm using sizes 2–3 (3–3¼mm) needles.

OTHER ROWAN YARNS

Rowan Pure Wool 4ply knits to the same gauge/tension as **Rowan 4ply Soft** using size 3 (3¼mm needles). A 100 percent superwash wool, it comes in 50g balls, each of which is approx 174yd/160m.

Rowan Felted Tweed Aran (50 percent merino, 50 percent alpaca, 25 percent viscose) knits to the same gauge/tension as **Rowan Yorkshire Tweed Aran** using size 8 (5mm) needles. **Rowan Felted Tweed Aran** comes in 50g balls, each of which is approx 95yd/87m.

Rowan Scottish Tweed Chunky (100 percent pure wool) knits to the same gauge/tension as **Rowan Yorkshire Tweed Aran** using size 11 (8mm) needles. Approx 109yd/100m per 100g ball.

Rowan Scottish Tweed 4ply (100 percent pure wool) knits to the same gauge/tension as **Rowan Yorkshire Tweed 4ply** using size 2–3 (3–3¼mm) needles. Approx 120yd/110m per 25g ball.